PRAISE FOR

I Dared to Hope

"Infused with the power of the Holy Spirit, Oscar radiates unrelenting hope. He views the world through the lens of possibility, focusing on a future unshackled by the prejudices, scores, and mistakes of the past. McCloud's understated manner, dry humor, and willingness to extend mutual friendship opened the doors of many strangers and continues to do so to this day. Oscar McCloud is a remarkably well-rounded, fully measured man. Take the time to get to know him."

—HALSEY KNAPP,
Senior Partner at Krevolin & Horst LLC

"Oscar's story is dramatic evidence that hope and faith can overcome even the most dire and unpromising circumstances. It is also a reminder that providing an opportunity to a young person can flower into an incredible result that benefits all of us. And I must admit I started reading and could not stop."

—TOM HOLCOMB,
retired attorney and partner at McLain & Merritt, Atlanta Legal Aid volunteer

"Oscar's life is a prime example of 'it does not matter where or under what circumstance you enter this world, what matters is how you decide to live it.' Every university should have this memoir on its reading list for first-time college students. This book will provide them with many 'yes you can' moments that will lead to a life filled with opportunities, just like Oscar's."

— **DR. MELVIN STITH,**
Dean Emeritus of Whitman School of Management at Syracuse University

"Few Presbyterian and ecumenical institutions have Oscar's creative fingerprints. He has been central to many of the social justice movements, not just within the PC(USA), but around the world. This book is an invitation to walk through history through his eyes and his experience. He has been a strong, kind, and imaginative leader throughout his ministry and I am honored to be his pastor and friend."

— **DR. SHANNON J. KERSHNER,**
Pastor of Central Presbyterian Church, Atlanta, Ga.

"Stories like this remind us why every generation ought to listen to those who came before them. Oscar tells his journey with the warmth and candor of someone speaking across the table to an old friend, and offers a clear window into how people lived, persevered, and moved forward. This must-read, inspirational memoir offers encouragement and stays with you long after the final page."

— **HENRY PRUITT, EDD.,**
former middle school principal, Teaneck, N.J.

I Dared to Hope

How a Passion For Justice
Transformed a Sharecropper's Son

J. OSCAR MCCLOUD

Published by Ripples Media

www.ripples.media

Atlanta, Georgia

First printing 2026

Cover design by Nicole Wedekind
Typesetting by Najdan Mancic

ISBN 978-1-971718-19-4 Paperback
ISBN 978-1-971718-20-0 Hardback
ISBN 978-1-971718-18-7 eBook
Library of Congress Control Number on file.

Dedicated to my daughters,

Michelle and Cassandra McCloud,

my grandson, Jerome Wessely,

and my wife, Kathy McCloud

"May the God of hope fill you with all joy and
peace in believing, so that you may abound
in hope by the power of the Holy Spirit."

ROMANS 15:13

TABLE OF CONTENTS

Introduction 1

  1. Life on Quaker Road 3

  2. A Doorway to a New Life 13

  3. More White Folks Than I Had Ever Known 26

  4. God Has Made of One Blood All People 34

  5. An Introduction To A Wider World 43

  6. Equipping Myself for Ministry 50

  7. Ordained and Called 63

  8. At the Heart of the Movement 87

  9. New Occasions, New Duties 107

 10. Preparing Our Successors 135

 11. Never Say 'Never' 143

 12. And Then Along Came Kathy 161

Conclusion 167

Appendix: A Guide To Presbyterianism 169

Acknowledgements 171

About the Author 172

INTRODUCTION

AT THE TIME OF MY birth, there was no evidence to suggest that I could anticipate a life marked by prominence or even modest achievement. I was the seventh child of a poor, Black sharecropping family surrounded by other poor people of color on a plantation in rural Georgia during the Great Depression.

Ninety years later, the possibility that my wife, Kathy, and I could now be living in comfortable retirement and overlooking the city of Atlanta from a condominium on Peachtree Street borders on the unimaginable. Indeed, the story of my passage from Burke County to Buckhead is so unlikely that it could easily be misconstrued as fiction. However, it is true, and I finally have yielded to the encouragement of friends and colleagues who coaxed me to share it.

My journey has carried me to educational institutions in Appalachia and New York City, enabled me to be of service to the Presbyterian church in the South and then around the world, and deepened my understanding of Africa, Asia, Europe, and Latin America, as well as my own country.

As the title of this memoir affirms, at the heart of my experiences there has been a reliance upon hope. Søren Kierkegaard, the Danish philosopher, observed that hope is a passion for the possible—a feeling to which all of us are entitled. For whatever reason—first as a child and then in later years—I was able to envision a different and fuller way of living and to move in the direction of that life.

I came to understand that what I was feeling went beyond wishful thinking or naïve optimism. Rather, it was a settled confidence in the promises of God. My watchword became the admonition from the Apostle Paul to the church in Rome: "May the God of hope fill you with joy and peace in believing, so that you may abound in hope by the power of the Holy Spirit."

My initial escape from the surroundings of my birth and childhood was through church-sponsored educational institutions in multi-racial settings. That experience opened my eyes to the possibility of service to the Christian church and particularly a Presbyterian denomination. Although initially called and ordained to parish ministry, I soon found myself on a career track that also included national and then international ecumenical service. Before retirement from active duty, I had the privilege of traveling to many sectors of the earth, meeting some of the world's prominent leaders, and helping to give direction to major denominational activity.

As it is important to remember, nothing that I will describe would have been possible without the support and encouragement of men and women who themselves helped to bring about positive change all over the earth.

It has been both a heady and humbling experience, for which I am profoundly grateful.

1

Life on Quaker Road

Y EARS AGO, A SECTION OF WAYNESBORO, the government seat of Burke County in eastern Georgia, was designated as the burial ground for an uncounted number of nameless and enslaved African Americans who once labored on the region's large cotton plantations. By the time I was born in 1936, human slavery in the United States had been officially abolished for seven decades. Nonetheless, the living and working conditions of Black people in that region had not undergone a great deal of change. An already wretched region of the country was still trying to extricate itself from the deep hole of the Great Depression, and we dark-skinned citizens were trapped at the bottom of that pit.

Put most plainly, we were very poor. It was simply a way of life.

If you are not familiar with Burke County, established in 1777, you probably never raised prize-winning English setters and pointers or brought them to the annual field trials in Waynesboro—known to those breeders as the Bird Dog Capital of the World. (Need I note that not many Black citizens are engaged in that pastime?)

My birthplace was an unpainted shack constructed of bare wooden planks. It stood scarcely five feet from Quaker Road, four miles outside of Waynesboro. During Colonial times the road had been a major thoroughfare, suitable for wheeled vehicles. It connected Savannah to a small, now-vanished settlement of Society of Friends members in McDuffie County, about 50 miles north of us. We knew the aged artery only as an unpaved slash of red clay across the countryside, almost impassable during rainy weather.

I was the seventh and last child of George and Sophronia McCloud. As my mother had done with all my siblings, she gave birth to me in our house with the assistance of Mrs. Julia Smith, a local midwife.

Our family knew very little about its history. We had no record of our forbearers; no research by Henry Louis Gates to explain our origins. My parents were married in 1924 while still very young. The six children in the family before I arrived were Tom, Willie, George Jr., Elijah, Viola, and Lucy.

My father was an illiterate sharecropper who planted,

cultivated, and harvested cotton, corn, and peanuts on a 75-acre portion of the Ivanhoe Plantation. That entire estate was the ancestral home of Paul Dye—someone about whom I have no charitable memories. (Let my ambivalent epitaph for him simply be, "May his soul rest in a cool place!")

Dye's family history was one that he shared with many other white landowners in that part of Georgia. It included tales of Union troops destroying Southern homesteads during General Sherman's famous march across the state. That demolition was seemingly never to be forgotten or forgiven—perhaps almost as painful to those Georgians as the legal eradication of slavery.

Until he was more than 70 years old, my dad never traveled farther from home than Augusta, some 30 miles away. The fact that he could neither read nor write makes it even more astounding that this septuagenarian managed a round trip on public transportation by himself to visit one of my mother's sisters in Philadelphia, Pennsylvania.

He could count but did not know how to do mathematical calculations. That deficiency put him at the mercy of the plantation owner when it was time to assess and disburse our family's share of the meager payment for our labors. My father was credited with only half of the crop he raised. From that total the owner deducted rent and any charges (with interest) for supplies he had sold to us. Small wonder that my father felt uncomfortable in the company of white people. Virtually all of their behavior to him highlighted their superior attitude.

The primary responsibility of keeping us fed and clothed fell to my mother. She cooked on a wood-burning stove that Southerners refer to as having four "eyes" (burners), and she did the "wash" by hand behind the house, loosening the dirt from filthy work garb on a corrugated metal washboard. The very limited amount of dry goods my parents could afford to purchase for our clothing or bedding came from Joe Goldberg, a Jewish merchant in town.

Both my mother and her children, once we reached school age, were expected to assist with planting, weeding (also known as chopping), and harvesting the cotton and other crops.

My first home had no insulation and no artificial light until rural electrification came to our area when I was a teenager. Such limited heat as we did enjoy on cold days came from a wood-burning fireplace. We had no indoor plumbing; our water came from a well, and our toilet facilities were an outhouse about one hundred feet from our dwelling.

In addition to the kitchen area where we ate our meals, the rest of the house consisted of two bedrooms. My parents and sisters slept in one of them; my brothers and I occupied the other. (Black Boy, our pet dog who was blind in one eye, slept on the small porches attached to the front and back of the building.)

To supplement the meager cash that my father earned, we raised chickens, hogs, and a couple of cows, and we grew our own vegetables. My father designated a row in the garden where I was permitted to sow and tend the plants I chose to grow. Although meant to be a chore, the experience instilled in me a love of gardening that I never lost.

When I was born, the family had been living in our dilapidated dwelling for 15 years, and we remained there until I reached high school age. Then we moved to a slightly larger house, shaded by pine trees, about one-half mile from Quaker Road. At the same time, we also acquired a car—a gift from one of my older brothers. Until he received that present, my father used an old bicycle that he purchased to travel around the immediate area.

Before the acquisition of an automobile, though, our family transportation was dependent upon two mules. The plantation owner provided those animals for farming purposes, but they also pulled us to town in our wagon on Saturdays and to Sunday services at the churches we attended.

As a child of God-fearing Baptists, I spent a lot of time in worship services—a lot of time! Each of at least three of the Black Baptist churches in our section of Burke County scheduled only one Sunday service every month, and my family attended all of them. No one held services on the first Sunday, but on the second Sunday we would worship at my father's church, Forest Hill Baptist. The next week we would be at Beechwood Baptist, and then on the fourth Sunday, we were regular attendees at Antioch Baptist, my mother's congregation. August was the season for revivals when we would go to hear visiting preachers almost every night.

I was baptized by immersion when I was 12 years old. To prepare for that ritual, I practiced holding my breath face down in a tub of water as long as possible. I was especially grateful when I learned that the ceremony was going to take place in a church whose congregation had constructed its own baptistry; it meant that I was not going to be "dunked" in a cold stream or smelly pond.

Even as a young boy I found it difficult to feel comfortable in any of those churches. The preachers were generally uneducated and not especially good leaders of their congregations. Their sermons consisted of more "whoopin' and hollerin'" than thoughtful instruction about Christian life. Emotional call-and-response exchanges between the pulpit and the pews overcame logic. Central to all of the messages from their preachers was a focus upon the centrality of Jesus's bodily resurrection and the goal of following him into an eternal after-life.

As I grew older, it was not lost on me that church members often seemed to have theological or organizational disagreements with their fellow congregants. They tended to resolve their differences by withdrawing their memberships and forming new churches—thus encouraging the proliferation of small congregations throughout rural areas of the South.

All the laborers on the Dye plantation were Black sharecroppers or day laborers. They were treated with only minimal friendliness or respect by their white supervisors, were never addressed by their last names, and were subject to cursing and even physical abuse.

On occasion that kind of harsh treatment extended even to children. I still am haunted by a vividly painful memory of an incident I witnessed when I was 12 years old. A young Black girl was chopping cotton with several other workers, including members of my family. When she failed to do her job to the satisfaction of the white overseer, he angrily left the field and returned with the plantation owner. That adult then beat her hard enough with a thick stick to leave scar tissue on her body.

My early formal schooling was meager. Like my brothers and sisters, I walked two miles from our home to a dilapidated building with one room that served seven grades. It constituted the only public education that was available to Black, elementary school children in our area. Our teacher, Mrs. Sally Griffin, did her best to share with us all that she knew, but she had not completed her own high school education. Each summer she would enroll in classes at Savannah State College, a historically Black institution, to expand her knowledge and strengthen her instructional skills. I have clear memories of the times I would assist her by helping to teach the younger children.

My parents' desire for their children to be educated received an important boost from the presence in the county of Boggs Academy. Boggs had been established in 1906 by the Presbyterian Church USA as a mission enterprise for poor rural Black children. Its name honored Virginia Boggs, the Corresponding Secretary of the Board of Missions for the Freedman. It had a deserved reputation for excellence. Four of my siblings had already been enrolled in that boarding school with a Black faculty and staff.

Nevertheless, after finishing seven grades of public instruction, I convinced my parents to permit me to attend the segregated Black high school in Waynesboro. My rationale for this desire had nothing to do with educational values. Rather, I was captivated by the thought of a daily ride in a school bus—the same kind of transportation enjoyed by the children who attended all-white institutions. (The "Black" school bus I rode was owned and driven by an African American garage owner and mechanic whom the local authorities hired for that purpose.) Even the need to board the bus at 6:30 a.m. failed to deter my interest in this plan. My parents approved my proposal with the understanding that I would transfer to

Boggs Academy after three years of attending the segregated public school.

The high school education that Burke County grudgingly provided for its Black young people was characterized by scarcity and neglect. Its sparse course outline, oriented primarily toward agriculture for the boys and home economics for the girls, was spread across grade eight through eleven—and did not include a twelfth grade until 1950. The main building housed a miniscule principal's office and four classrooms through which students rotated. Such science instruction as there was took place in an adjoining barracks-like structure that had two microscopes for the use of several hundred students. Since the institution did not have an auditorium, it could schedule no school assemblies. The primary extra-curricular activity involved organizing a basketball team that competed with other Black schools in the area.

Yet, thanks to dedicated faculty members, it was possible for a student to learn, even in that deprived setting. My English teacher, the wife of the school principal, was a graduate of Atlanta University, a historically Black institution. It was she who introduced me to the writings of Paul Laurence Dunbar, Langston Hughes, and Arna Bontemps. From another instructor I learned about Black scientists and inventors like Benjamin Banneker.

Nonetheless, by the time I completed my public-school studies, I was sufficiently disappointed by the education I had received that I was ready to make the move to Boggs Academy.

It is a tribute to our parents' encouragement and to their offsprings' own diligence that all of the McCloud children escaped from plantation life. After graduation from the segregated high school in Waynesboro, Tom left for Washington, DC, and secured a job with the telephone company (with which he remained until his retirement). Willie finished his schooling at Boggs Academy, studied further at Fort Valley State College, (another historically Black institution) and then entered military service. George, Jr. after high school relocated to Augusta, Georgia, and then Cincinnati, Ohio, where he spent much of the rest of his life doing construction. Elijah completed the Boggs curriculum and went into the U.S. Air Force. Viola enrolled at historically Black Paine College in Augusta, Georgia, to begin her preparation for a career in nursing, and Lucy graduated from Barber-Scotia College, yet another historically Black college founded by the Presbyterian Church USA in Concord, North Carolina, and became a teacher.

2

A Doorway to a New Life

L EADERS OF THE PROTESTANT REFORMATION placed a high value upon literacy; both John Calvin and John Knox established systems of public education in Switzerland and Scotland. Presbyterians brought that tradition with them to the New World and created schools for white students throughout the new United States. They also were among the first to organize educational institutions for the former enslaved people after slavery was abolished. It was that latter motivation that prompted the formation of Boggs Academy.

The mailing address for Boggs was Keysville, Georgia. However, the school was situated in the country, nine miles from that tiny town. The choice of location was highly deliberate. Boggs came into being during a period in Southern history of extreme white hostility toward African Americans. In September 1906, the same month during which the new school opened, white residents of Atlanta carried out an unprovoked massacre of Black citizens in that city.

The founder of Boggs was a Black Presbyterian minister, the Rev. John Phelps, a graduate of Biddle University in Charlotte, North Carolina (later renamed Johnson C. Smith University). His school's first "campus" consisted of two acres of donated farmland. On that property he erected a chapel (Morgan Grove Presbyterian Church) that initially doubled as a classroom building. During the next eight decades, Boggs steadily acquired additional property and constructed enough buildings to house and educate about 200 students each year. After a fire destroyed the original sanctuary in 1987, a generous family from Philadelphia underwrote the construction of a new worship center. John I. Blackburn Presbyterian Church was named after one of the donors.

Boggs, which had opened with five students, initially was intended to respond to the educational needs of the poorest Black children in the Burke County region. However, reports about its reputation for academic excellence began to spread. Soon it was steadily attracting increased enrollment by the daughters and sons of African American families around the country as well as international students.

Boggs had classrooms, dormitories, a dining hall, a gym, a shop, cottages for faculty and staff, and an athletic field. (Given the poverty of my background, it perhaps should come as no surprise to learn that in this upscale setting I had my first encounter with indoor showers and flush toilets.)

The school day began with compulsory chapel or assembly attendance. Classes concluded at 4 p.m. We had to be in our dormitories by 9:30 p.m. and in bed by ten o'clock.

Boggs also had established the tradition of training excellent choirs that specialized in *a capella* singing and frequently won the choral competitions in which they competed. (I still remember our arrangement of "Jesu, Joy of Man's Desiring".)

The choral contests in which we competed were often held at the Ballard Hudson High School in Macon, one of the outstanding institutions for Black students at that time. For those of us coming from schools in rural counties, the experience was akin to visiting a sophisticated college campus.

Our best-loved faculty member was the choir director, Charles Francis. He also was the social studies teacher and Assistant Principal, later becoming the Principal after Harold Stinson left to assume the presidency of Stillman College in Tuscaloosa, Alabama. The love and admiration for Mr. Francis was derived from his manner of giving all students the same down-to-earth respect and affection, regardless of family background or condition. He always had time to counsel us, treating each as someone with unique needs and gifts. We all felt as if we were his own children.

When I wasn't attending classes or singing in the choir, much of my time was devoted to "earning my keep." We students paid for our tuition and/or developed agricultural skills by milking cows, feeding hogs and goats, and preserving the vegetables we grew. Long before the concept became popular, we were producing farm-to-table meals. All of us spent at least one class period each day washing dishes in the kitchen, sweeping floors, cleaning classrooms, mowing lawns, or tending livestock.

As already described, my early religious education—such as it was—had occurred within the atmosphere of rural Baptist churches. Becoming acquainted at Boggs with what Protestants call the "Reformed Tradition" was a liberating experience. Already attracted to neatness and well-organized behavior, I immediately felt drawn to my new school's way of doing things. Presbyterians, as I quickly learned, abhor disarray and confusion. Their favorite Biblical citation may well be the verse from 1 Corinthians (14:40) that states "but let all things be done decently and in order." For the denomination sometimes referred to as God's "frozen chosen," thought trumps emotion. Its members live by—no, thrive on—order, and they are renowned for their allegiance to it. Indeed, the second chapter of the Constitution of the Presbyterian Church (U.S.A.) is titled *The Book of Order*; it governs the way that its members are supposed to worship and to conduct their organizational business.

The Presbyterian worship that I came to know and appreciate included a balance of scripture reading, prayer, communal singing, the sacraments of baptism and communion, an offering, and a closing charge to the congregation to serve the world. It was generally liturgical but not overly ceremonial, often blending traditional and contemporary elements.

Another major difference from my previous experience was an educational emphasis upon living the Christian life. Presbyterians seemed to care more about following the Golden Rule than climbing some golden stairs into a heavenly afterlife. I was further impressed by the Biblical knowledge of the visiting pastors whom I heard preach in the Boggs chapel. Finally, as I became increasingly acquainted with my new denomination, I appreciated its involvement of youth and its advancement of women in leadership roles.

All of these factors solidified my decision to become a Presbyterian. Since I already had been baptized, I joined my new denomination by a simple reaffirmation of faith in the campus church in 1953. I don't remember the precise moment when it occurred, but at some point, during my time at Boggs, I further determined that I wanted to become a Presbyterian pastor.

Have I since then had my quarrels with the Presbyterian church? Of course I have, particularly over issues having to do with race and social justice. Did I ever regret the decision to join the denomination? No. The path I chose to follow while still in high school remained clear.

Memory of my "conversion" leads me to recall an incident when I was chosen to stand in the place of the pastor for the filming of a promotion for the school. I was stationed outside the church entrance, greeting the attendees as they left worship. My instructions were to keep my back to the camera so no one would see my face, but I felt that I nonetheless carried myself ministerially.

The daily calendar at Boggs was filled with activity, but it still left room for pubescent adolescents to pursue relationships with other girls and boys. One dating option at Boggs was attendance at film screenings, during which young couples were permitted to sit together.

Although sixteen years old, I was still shy in the presence of girls and usually lacked the courage to introduce myself to them face-to-face. However, I was always ready to make advances with notes and cards that proclaimed my interest. My favorite technique was to quote the appropriate lyrics from hit songs. (Remember Nat "King" Cole singing, "They tried to tell us we're too young"?).

In the fall of 1952, while lounging on the school lawn, I watched Robbie Foster stroll across the campus. I immediately felt a powerful attraction to that lovely, full-figured, dark-skinned tenth grader. She was in the company of a male upperclassman; it was not the first time I had seen them together. Resorting to my standard operating procedure, I sent her a note. Was she seriously involved with that young man? I inquired. After several days, she responded with a message of her own: if I was asking whether I might become her boyfriend, her answer was "yes." And so began a teenage romance that continued for the next two years.

Her full name was Robbie Juanita Foster. She came from a financially comfortable family in Bremen, Georgia—a predominantly white community near the Alabama state line. It was the home of the Sewell Clothing Company, a manufacturer of men's and women's clothing. As I got to know Robbie, I learned that her father had created an unusual but profitable business niche for himself. He purchased slightly damaged or irregular Sewell garments and re-sold them at discounted prices from the trunk of his car. That enterprise had been sufficiently successful to enable him to buy land from financially distressed owners around the county and accumulate significant property holdings.

One of the Boggs requirements for each junior-year student was to prepare an "oration." The assignment involved selecting and researching a topic, outlining, and then composing an essay on the subject, memorizing the presentation, and reciting it before a class of approximately 25 students. The faculty would then select five or six of the best orations to be delivered to a larger audience in the next year.

My ambitious 1953 presentation was titled, "Negro in History". Using an old manual typewriter with which I had little familiarity, I used two fingers to pound out, laboriously, a two-page, 700-word document. It was replete with strike-overs and featured a few spelling mistakes. However, what it may have lacked in appearance it made up with fervor.

"NEGRO IN HISTORY"

May I first say that we do not know precisely when the history of our race began, but we do know that it has had an upward trend. It was said by Booker T. Washington, a Negro educator, and I quote, "one of the most fundamental and far-reaching deeds that has been accomplished during the last quarter of a century has been that by which [the] Negro has been helped to find himself and to learn the secret of civilization. It has been necessary for the Negro to learn the difference between being worked and working to learn that being worked meant degradation, while work means civilization: that all forms of labor are honorable, and all forms of idleness disgraceful."

Mr. Webster defines History as the branch of knowledge that records and explains past events as steps in human progress."Negro history" probably began many years before the year of 1865. During the years of slavery in most cases if a Southern White man wanted a house built, he consulted a Negro mechanic about the plans and the actual building structure. If he wanted a suit of clothes made he went to a Negro tailor, and for shoes he went to a shoemaker of the same race. In a certain way every slave plantation in the South was an industrial school. On these plantations young men and women were constantly being trained not only as farmers but as carpenters, blacksmiths, wheelwrights, brick masons, engineers, dietitians, laundresses, and housekeepers. Today, we still have Negroes who are outstanding in those fields. As the years past from slavery on into a stage of freedom our race have acquired people who became outstanding lawyers, contractors, architectors, political leaders, educators, and many others. Our race in "Negro history "stands out for it[s] so many contributions in so few years.

Some of our past Negroes who are outstanding in history are those like Benjamin Banneker, the inventor of the clock that we use, Booker T. Washington, the founder and first Principal of the Tuskegee Institute, George W. Carver, a chemist, once professor at Tuskegee Institute. He discovered oil in the peanut. Dr. Charlotte

H. Brown, educator and founder of The Charlotte H. Brown Institute. In the present time we have Negroes who are leaders in the same positions as those in the past, only along with them we have many in new fields. As members of the U.N. (United Nations), Such as Dr. Ralph H. Bunche, United Nations Mediator and Trusteeship director. Mary McC. Bethune, an educator and founder of Bethune-Cookman College, Daytona Beach, Fla. Walter White, Secretary of the NAACP. Paul N. Magloire, President of Haiti, And those in the sport field such as Jackie Robinson, Joe Louis and many others. In the writing field we have such as Langston Hughes, and Frank Yerby, a native of Augusta. Ga.

The future Negroes in history must come from the youth of today. If we do not strive to reach the highest peak possible in life we will be permitting the trend of increase to become a trend [of] decrease, which no race, nation, or country wishes to prosess. We, as youth of today and the future Negroes in history must strive to obtain the training that is necessary to bring our race up from where our parents left it.

Today the world is asking for the man who has already obtain[ed] the ability to do a job and not for the man that is trying to learn. If we as youth do not improve that which our ancestors provided for us, we are asking for a downward trend in the history of our race. We must take a greater step than that which was taken by our foreparents, so we will improve the standards for our prosterities.

May I conclude by saying that in our history "Negro History" we have many people who are not in such fields as medicine, religion, business enterprises, political leaders, and also in farming, which is very important in "Negro history." To achieve recognition as many of those I have briefly spoken of, we must do as George W. Carver, quoted in an issue of "Practice English" and I quote, "start where you are with what you have; make something of it; never be satisfied" unquote. May I leave this question with you will you wait for opportunity to knock, or will you go out to meet it?

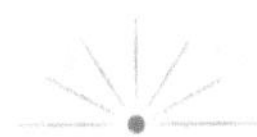

The Boggs philosophy and curriculum inspired academic ambition. We students were encouraged to envision and pursue education beyond high school. As an example, on one occasion, Robbie, two other classmates and I were taken on a motivational visit to the historically Black graduate school, Atlanta University. Dear Old BA [Boggs Academy], as the school song described the institution, did its best to prepare me for an ascent into the world of higher education—a possibility that would once have seemed unlikely if not impossible.

Boggs also exposed its students to other educational experiences in the fields of music, science and sports, mainly in Georgia. Some of these opportunities occurred at Paine College in the city of Augusta. That institution for African Americans had been jointly founded by the leadership of the white Methodist Episcopal Church South, (now the United Methodist Church), and the Colored Methodist Episcopal Church (now the Christian Methodist Episcopal Church).

Although I had been quite attracted to Robbie Foster, the teenage infatuation that began in tenth grade did not survive our departure from Boggs. A year after I graduated, she finished high school and became a student at Hampton Institute, the famous historically Black college in Virginia. However, she stayed there for only one year before transferring to Lane College, another African American institution in Jackson, Tennessee. Sometime during that period our correspondence with each other stopped, and I resumed my pursuit of relationships with other young women.

The Boggs Academy experience most certainly had provided me with new layers of learning and sophistication, refinement, and confidence. Nonetheless, as I was to discover, the world that awaited my arrival was still quick to remind me of my place in it. An important lesson occurred when three of us recent Boggs graduates went looking for summer employment. Like many other Black high school and college students from the South in those days, Ermest Latimore, Willard Jackson, and I were employed as pickers by the Imperial Tobacco Company in Windsor, Connecticut. While in New England, I had my first unpleasant experience with a Northern version of racial discrimination—a phenomenon that the author Oscar Brown had described as "Up South"—what Black people hoping to escape Jim Crow discovered in the North.

In Georgia, as in much of the South, I was more accustomed to the legal separation of Black and white people from each other than to a more nuanced discrimination on the basis of color. In Waynesboro, for example, we had both white and Black restaurants and other businesses. Based on the color of your skin, you knew exactly which establishment to frequent...or not to frequent.

However, in Windsor, where I could locate only one barber shop, its white proprietor simply refused to serve me because, as he put it, "I don't cut colored folks' hair."

3

*More White Folks Than
I Had Ever Known*

B OTH MY FAMILY AND I wanted me to continue my education. But where and how? Even the few historically Black colleges about which we knew like Barber-Scotia and Fort Valley State were beyond our financial reach. Nonetheless, we discovered that answers to our questions could be found at an institution in the Swannanoa Valley of North Carolina, about 10 miles east of Asheville.

It was yet another education-oriented mission venture of the Presbyterian Church, USA, started in 1894 as the Asheville Farm School for boys from the Appalachian region. In 1942 it merged with the Dorland-Bell School, a Presbyterian academy for young women in Hot Springs,

North Carolina. Then, taking the name of a former Secretary of Rural Church Work for the Board of National Missions, the merged venture became Warren Wilson Junior College.

A singular attraction of that institution was its comprehensive work-study program that dignified physical labor while underwriting the cost of a college education. Students paid for their schooling, room, and board by performing jobs in food service, the laundry, a farm that raised cows and hogs, building construction and maintenance, and a forestry program. Half of the students worked half of each day while the rest attended classes. Then they switched roles.

I applied and was accepted. This arrangement with Warren Wilson was not just to my benefit. In a sense, the school also needed me. The newly legalized racial integration of higher education was slow in coming to western North Carolina. Arthur Bannerman, the college president, had not been highly successful in recruiting Black students. The institution had thus far admitted only one African-American girl, Georgia Powell, who came from Boggs Academy. Alma Shippy, who was from the Swannanoa vicinity, was the first Black male in the school's history, but he stayed for just one year. However, Bannerman arranged with Harold Stinson, the Principal of Boggs, for me to become Shippy's replacement and recruited another young woman—Marjorie Lewis.

It took a while for me to become accustomed to being in the company of more white people than I had ever known and whom I certainly was not inclined to trust. Further adding to the population mix was the presence of international students. (I had never before laid eyes on an Hispanic individual, let alone anyone from Finland, Iran, Lebanon, Greece, or Thailand.)

Not just the school but also the outside community was overwhelmingly Caucasian. I soon concluded that mountain people were not burdened with the racist heritage of having owned large plantations that were worked by enslaved laborers. These white folks tended to treat us few African Americans with more curiosity or nervousness than animosity and fear. I don't recall encountering any overt racial prejudice on campus.

When the "whiteness" of Warren Wilson would begin to feel too oppressive, though, I could take a bus or attempt to hitchhike into Asheville. The larger town's appeal had little to do with its cultural or recreational offerings. Rather, it was the home of the United Methodist Church's Allen School for Girls, a boarding institution for young African American women that had earned a reputation for academic excellence. Asheville also was the place where I could get a haircut.

There were other significant differences between the Swannanoa Valley in which Warren Wilson was situated and the East Georgia region in which I had been raised. The farms and plantations of Burke County spread across rolling hills. On a clear day at Warren Wilson, it was possible to look up and see Mount Mitchell (the highest point east of the Mississippi River whose summit I visited several times) from the campus. Other smaller but still towering peaks of forested-mountains surrounded us. Each year, the college would suspend classes so faculty and students could celebrate "Mountain Day" by hiking to a high-altitude picnic.

The campus itself was a bucolic wonder through which flowed the Swannanoa River. The property incorporated a farm with several hundred acres, many more acres of woodland, miles of hiking trails, and pastures and pens for cows and pigs.

Guiding the educational process and setting the tone of tolerance at Warren Wilson was a dedicated and underpaid faculty. Many of them lived in campus housing and were readily available to students. Especially memorable to me was Fred Ohler, who had first come south from Yale Divinity School for an internship year. After graduation from seminary, he returned to Swannanoa as the Warren Wilson chaplain and remained there for the rest of his career—a continual source of counsel and guidance for all who sought his assistance. Also meriting special mention is his wife, Beverly. A gifted author and artist, she was a lovely and charming hostess at the frequent gatherings in the living room of the Ohler apartment.

The social life for the fewer than 300 students was limited. I learned folk dancing, (quickly determining that the principal skill needed for this popular recreation was the ability to count). I also sang in the choir (careful to stand next to someone who could read music), and I went to the occasional movie on campus. Dating was not a common practice. Perhaps that is why I still carry the awkward memory of being interrupted by Barbara Hempleman, a faculty member, who found me "petting" with a white co-ed. The girl had a reputation for being overly generous with her affections, and the professor gently suggested that my companion probably would not be helpful to my future. (Dr. Hempleman and I became friends and maintained that relationship long after I graduated from Warren Wilson.)

If truth be known, I didn't have a lot of time to fool around; I was up against the toughest academic challenge of my young life. As just one example of the educational rigor I now faced, I had never learned anything beyond basic algebra at Boggs. Consequently, I was required to take a basic math course at Warren Wilson.

Perhaps the most ironic feature of my matriculation at Warren Wilson surfaced with my first job on campus: this boy from a Georgia plantation for whom feeding hogs had once been a daily chore was assigned to clean the piggery! However, there was no way that I could interpret that dirty work as a racial slur once I discovered that I would be working side-by-side with Dale Watson, a white Indiana farmer's son. Clearly, the school was taking advantage of our unique backgrounds in the field of porcine management.

As we came to know each other, Dale shared with me the information that his roommate had departed. He further explained that he did not enjoy living alone across the hall from the smoking room that usually was filled with noisy students.

I too had a single room, across the hall from the dormitory matron. It was my strong suspicion that I had been intentionally isolated to protect me. The college, I theorized, did not want me to experience the kind of negative reaction from a white roommate that the first African American male to be admitted to the college may have encountered the previous year.

Dale suggested that the two of us should become roommates. After the matron confirmed my willingness to approve this arrangement, we moved in together and have remained friends to this day.

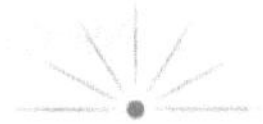

During the summer of 1955, at the end of my first academic year at Warren Wilson, I remained on campus and worked in the dairy—attaching milking machines to a herd of Holstein cows every morning and evening and emptying the frothy liquid they produced into 10-gallon stainless steel cans.

The second year in Swannanoa was more routine than the first. I studied; I completed my various other jobs which included pruning pine trees; I attended worship in the log chapel on campus every Wednesday morning, and I went to vesper services on Sunday evenings.

And then, all too quickly, the Warren Wilson experience also was behind me. My brother Willie, who was teaching agriculture at Boggs Academy, and his wife, Bessie, who taught English there, drove up from Georgia to attend my graduation.

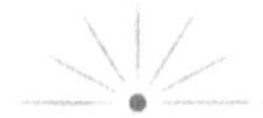

Six decades later, Warren Wilson (by then a four-year college) honored me with an invitation to be the speaker for the institution's celebration of the Martin Luther King, Jr. holiday. Reflecting aloud about what my two years there had meant to my development, I talked about the importance of the hope and courage that my time in Swannanoa had helped me to fashion and nurture. Clearly, Warren Wilson was an essential launching pad for the next step in my development.

Other former students too have readily praised the institution for its role in their success. Two years ahead of me was Billy Edd Wheeler, a poor white boy from the coal mining section of West Virginia. He learned about the small junior college from a Presbyterian missionary who visited his hometown of Highcoal. In later life, Wheeler described Warren Wilson as "not a preparation for the world but the good world itself." He went on to achieve fame as the songwriter of hits like "Jackson" (recorded by Johnny Cash and June Carter) and "Coward of the County" (premiered by Kenny Rogers) and to become a member of the Nashville Songwriters Hall of Fame.

4

God Has Made of One Blood All People

DURING THE SPRING OF 1956, a group of us Warren Wilson students took a field trip to eastern Kentucky to visit Berea College. To participate I reluctantly had to decline the invitation from a very attractive Allen School student to escort her to a debutante ball. Nonetheless, it didn't take long for me to determine that I had made the right choice.

I was fascinated by what I learned. The institution had been a champion of social justice since its founding in 1855. Cassius Marcellus Clay, an abolitionist politician, had given a 10-acre tract of land in eastern Kentucky to his friend, the Reverend John Gregg Fee, to establish an inter-racial community. Fee built an anti-slavery church and a one-room schoolhouse whose teachers he recruited from the progressive Oberlin College in Ohio. He named this new settlement "Berea" after the Macedonian community whose members were among the early converts to Christianity (Acts 17:10). The motto of the college—which continues to the present—was "God has made of one blood all people."

Pro-slavery opposition forced the residents of Berea to leave, but they returned after the Civil War and re-established the institution. However, after nearly 40 years, the Kentucky legislature enacted a law that prohibited the teaching of Black and white students together. When that legislation was amended in 1950 to allow racial integration above the high school level, Berea became the first college in Kentucky to re-open its doors to African American students.

Berea also was the alma mater of Carter G. Woodson, known as the Father of Black History—someone about whom I first learned when I was composing my "oration" at Boggs Academy. Raised in rural Virginia, Woodson was the second African American (after W. E. B. DuBois) to earn a doctoral degree from Harvard University.

It was impossible not to be impressed by the contrasts between the admirable but small two-year institution I had been attending and the well-established, nationally recognized, four-year college to which I was introduced. The work-study program that helped to underwrite Berea's self-sufficiency was more comprehensive and organized than the one I had experienced at Warren Wilson. The college had its own hospital and physicians as well as a school of nursing and a fire department. It also operated a dairy, a bakery, and a printing operation that published a newspaper and produced promotional materials for the college. One of its most impressive features was its ownership and operation of a hotel—the Daniel Boone Tavern—with beautiful wooden furniture, much of it handcrafted by Berea's students.

What I saw at this remarkable institution in the mountains of eastern Kentucky convinced me to apply for admission. I was accepted and began to plan accordingly. As usual, one of the first orders of business had to involve finding additional financial support for my continued education. My search for a summer job landed me a position as a counselor at the Presbytery of Chicago's Camp Gray in Saugatuck, Michigan, on the shore of Lake Michigan.

A small group of African American and white college students began that summer experience with an orientation weekend in Chicago. We assembled at a Neighborhood House, a long-standing nonprofit facility. To sensitize us to racial dynamics in Illinois, the facility's director suggested that we all go to dinner in the city's downtown district known as The Loop. Before setting off, he warned us that we might encounter difficulties. As predicted, our interracial group was refused service, a reminder that we were "up South." Indeed, it was beginning to dawn on me that there might not be a place in the United States where a Black person could escape from racial discrimination.

Nevertheless, the rest of the summer proceeded smoothly. I had oversight responsibility for a series of campers—eight to ten junior high boys from Chicago's inner city. Each day we spent time at the lake, competed in athletic contests, and worked on crafts.

We also ate together, and I quickly learned that some of the boys were not accustomed to family-style meals. When the food arrived at the table, they would grab helpings of bread and other servings without waiting for them to be passed. It was clear that they feared that they wouldn't get their fair share. I may have been raised in poverty on a rural plantation, but I had acquired enough manners to impose some table etiquette on our mealtimes.

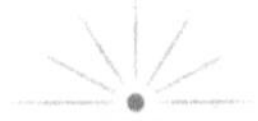

Upon arriving on the Berea campus that fall, I discovered that the college had enrolled approximately 35 African American undergraduates—still a modest total when compared to the days when the enrollment had been almost equally divided into Black and white students. (Interestingly, my first roommate was a Korean student who also had transferred from Warren Wilson.)

My beginning job was in the cafeteria, from which I was elevated to a janitorial position in one of the dormitories and eventually to the responsibility of being a resident assistant.

The college itself may have been a champion of liberal values, but life beyond the campus border was sadly lacking in racial tolerance. A notorious drugstore in the town of Berea refused to serve Black customers, and—sad to say—the college administration showed little inclination to challenge that blatant discrimination. In fact, many of the other business establishments were owned by the college and leased to racist proprietors. Going into town was not a pleasant experience for African Americans, and visits to Richmond, Kentucky, the next-largest town, offered little improvement. As a result, I looked forward to the few visits I enjoyed with my brother, George, in Cincinnati.

A greater personal challenge was the academic program. I was not an "A" student, so the coursework was even tougher than the challenges I had faced during my first two undergraduate years at Warren Wilson. Fortunately, I was willing to study and was further blessed by a dedicated faculty. Those remarkable professors were committed to their students' success and always seemed available to provide us with counseling and encouragement outside the classroom. They deserve major credit for the large number of Berean students who went to graduate school.

Standing in the way of my graduation was the fulfillment of two specific college requirements. The first was the demonstration that I could swim—a challenge that involved more courage than academic diligence. A morbid dread of drowning had terrified me since the time as a small boy when I slipped off a log while fishing with my brother and fell beneath the water. However, at Berea I finally conquered that fear sufficiently to be able to push myself away from one end of the swimming pool and paddle to the other.

The equally frightening challenge to be met was passing an oral examination in French. I had to demonstrate that I could understand questions put to me in that language and respond in similar fashion. My stomach was filled with "butterflies" throughout the ordeal, but I passed the exam and never again attempted to converse *en francais*.

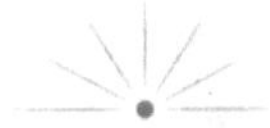

Among the faculty members who had a major impact upon my education and way of thinking was Roscoe "Rusty" Giffin. He was a Quaker who chaired the sociology department and spent nearly his entire career at Berea. He also was the first person to tell me about Koinonia Farm. The unique utopian community that had been established in rural southwest Georgia. Listening to his description, I made a mental note to find a way to visit this unusual experiment in communal living.

The opportunity for that experience came early during the summer of 1957 when I made my way by bus on my own to Americus, Georgia. It was an inspirational journey, primarily because Clarence Jordan, Koinonia's founder, was a remarkable man. Having earned a degree in agriculture from the University of Georgia, he had responded to a call to Christian ministry and next earned two degrees in theology. Then, in 1942, declining various offers to preach and to teach, this white Baptist minister, his family, and one other family established Koinonia Farm.

Their promotion of a radically Christian, communal, interracial life was anathema to the white people of the region. As I learned from my conversations with Jordan and other members of the community, the Koinonians were subject to persecution, prosecution, and economic boycotting of their agricultural products. Their espousal of pacifism at the height of World War II aroused further anger and helped to instigate their excommunication from the local Baptist church.

(Years later, however, their example inspired the formation of what became Habitat for Humanity. Also, the publication and subsequent dramatization of *The Cotton Patch Gospel,* a colloquial translation by Jordan of the gospels of Matthew and John, further attracted positive attention to the unique community.)

My trip to Koinonia had required me to change buses in Atlanta. During the layover, I succumbed to the impulse to place a telephone call to Robbie Foster, my high school girlfriend. We had been out of touch with each other for many months.

I reached her mother, who informed me that Robbie was having dental surgery and could not speak with me. As soon as I returned to Berea, though, I sent her a letter. She responded promptly and enclosed a recent photograph of herself. That picture awakened all my former feelings about her. Thus began a renewed relationship that lasted for the next four decades until her death.

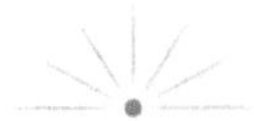

During the rest of that summer my college job called for me to open the gymnasium each evening and teach square dancing. Members of my family found the notion of a young Black man from rural Georgia instructing white mountain people in the intricacies of country dancing to be highly amusing. No doubt they were additionally entertained when they discovered that my occupational versatility also included cleaning the bathrooms in my dormitory.

During my final semester at Berea, I was reminded that much of the world into which I would soon be graduating did not share the idealistic values of the college. Professor Giffin drove home that lesson when he offered the six African American and white students—all Southerners—in his senior sociology seminar an alternative to a final written exam. Instead, he invited us to join him for a sit-in at a restaurant in the town of Berea. We accepted the challenge and, perhaps not surprisingly, were refused service. His last lesson to us was a clear reminder that the society into which we were graduating was still a world of disturbing bigotry.

Graduation came and went. Once again, members of my faithful and supportive family were in the audience for the ceremony. This time it was my mother, my brother, George, my sister, Viola, and Viola's daughter, Debra, who cheered for my receipt of a diploma.

5

An Introduction To A Wider World

I T WAS DURING MY TIME at Berea that I first learned about Operation Crossroads Africa. The organization's founder, James Robinson, came to the college to speak to the student body. A native of Knoxville, Tennessee, who had been raised in Ohio, he was a graduate of Lincoln University in Pennsylvania and Union Theological Seminary in New York.

His drive and enthusiasm were inspirational to all he met. Harry Emerson Fosdick, the renowned pastor of the Riverside Church, had been deeply impressed by the young minister—so much that he had encouraged Jim to become the pastor of the defunct Morningside Presbyterian Church on the western edge of Harlem. That congregation had abandoned its handsome Victorian-style church building during the Great Depression as its white members moved away and were replaced by Black residents. Robinson accepted the Fosdick challenge and successfully built a racially integrated membership of approximately 1,000 members that he re-named the Church of the Master.

However, his interest had now shifted to another passion: the future of post-Colonial Africa. Sharpening that focus were the friendships he had made at Lincoln University with two students who would emerge as African leaders: Kwaame Nkrumah, soon to become the first president of Ghana, and Nnamdi Azikiwe, Nigeria's first chief executive. In 1954, Robinson also undertook a tour of Africa on behalf of the Presbyterian Board of Foreign Missions. Later that year he set forth his impressions of the trip for the prestigious Lyman Beecher lectureship program at Yale University in a series of presentations titled "Adventurous Preaching in a World of Change and Trouble." His remarks promoted the idea of a program in which multi-racial groups of young people would build bridges of friendship to Africa.

I was so moved by the verbal picture of West Africa he painted for the Berean students that I approached him afterwards to express my interest in being part of his new program. After he invited me to put my thoughts in writing, I sent him a letter. In that message I also was quick to note that I could not afford to apply. His reply assured me that he would find the funds to pay for my participation.

It was my privilege to be in the first group of about 60 young people selected for participation in Robinson's new program. We assembled in New York City early in the summer of 1958 for orientation and training. Joining us as the group leader was the jovial Martin Luther Harvey, longtime Dean of Students at Southern University, the historically Black state school in Baton Rouge, Louisiana. We were housed at the Jewish Theological Seminary on Morningside Heights.

The city's many sights and a show at Radio City Music Hall impressed us, but several of us young men were equally fascinated by our discovery of Central Park. Slipping away from the rest of the group one night, we wandered through a portion of that darkened urban nature preserve. (My Brooklyn-based sister who had heard stories about the dangers that lurked in the park was horrified when she learned about our nocturnal exploits.)

Other experiences of our time in the city included being introduced by Jim to Eleanor Roosevelt, to Harrison Salisbury, the Pulitzer Prize-winning *New York Times* reporter, and to Mary Rockefeller, the wife of Nelson Rockefeller, the New York governor.

Still fixed firmly in my memory are my early ventures into the city's complex subway system and the cab driver who responded to my ten-cent tip by angrily throwing the dime that I gave him back at me.

I also took advantage of being in New York to visit the United Presbyterian Church headquarters. The primary purpose of that appointment was to explore (successfully, I should add) the possibility of receiving scholarship support for attending seminary.

All too soon it was time to leave for Africa. We boarded a four-engine, propellor-driven Pan American Clipper for a 26-hour trip that included stops for fuel and food in Boston, Newfoundland, the Azores, Lisbon, and Dakar, the capital city of Senegal.

After de-planing in Monrovia, the capital of Liberia, we were divided into several sub-groups and dispatched to work on projects for the next six weeks in Liberia, Ghana, Nigeria, Senegal, and Sierra Leone.

I had never left the United States, let alone set foot in a Third World country. Everything I saw and experienced was new and exciting.

During our orientation in New York, we learned that Liberia had been founded by the American Colonization Society in 1822 for the resettlement of freeborn Blacks and former slaves and that it was the oldest Black republic in the world after Haiti. However, words alone could not have prepared us for the beauty of the country's large forests or, on the other hand, the shortage of paved roads. We were covered with red dust by the time that the open Land Rover in which we traveled reached the village where we would be working.

The assignment of my group was to construct a one-room schoolhouse in a rural village near Cuttington College. Cuttington was an Episcopal mission enterprise in the central region of Liberia that had been in operation since 1889 and had educated many of the country's leaders. After the building was completed, it was going to be operated by the college which would assign its students to be classroom teachers.

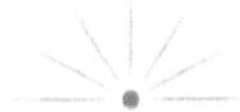

Burgess Carr, the student body president at the college, shared with us his intent to become the first Liberian bishop of that country's Episcopal Church. In later years he achieved his goal, and I maintained contact with him, primarily because of his involvement with the international ecumenical movement and the All-African Council of Churches.

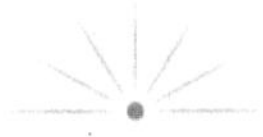

Our eleven-member team included both Black and white students from a variety of college and university backgrounds. One of us was Jamaican; another was Jewish. A tall, red-headed engineering undergraduate from UCLA was quickly designated as our construction expert. Since most of us spoke only English, we were fortunate that it was the official language of the country.

Four Tanzanian students who joined our group observed us with continual suspicion, trying to determine what had motivated us to come to Africa to do the work of unskilled laborers. Were we the children of wealthy parents seeking a new experience or perhaps employees of the United States government? It took a while to convince them that we were truly volunteers with good intentions.

We also were treated to a visit with William Vacanarat Shadrach Tubman, the nineteenth president of the country, at his country farm while he was hosting the president of the Firestone Tire and Rubber Company. That occasion included a tour of Firestone's natural rubber plantation, the world's largest operation of its kind. (President Tubman, by the way, was a direct descendant of the freed African slaves who had settled that section of Africa once known as the Pepper Coast.)

Crossroaders (as we came to be called) wrote letters and diaries describing our awe at African landscapes, the warmth of our hosts, and the joy of shared accomplishment. For many it was a season of "firsts": the first time mixing concrete, the first time eating fufu (a starchy native dish), the first time discussing politics beneath the stars of West Africa. To be sure, that summer's experience was not without its difficulties. Unfamiliar food, climate, and living conditions could pose challenges, and there were moments when the volunteers experienced homesickness, culture shock, and miscommunication. However, those times also nurtured resilience and empathy. I cannot think of any of us who were not profoundly changed by the experience. The ripple effect of what we went through together was long-lasting. Many of us went on to careers in international development, education, diplomacy, and other forms of global activism.

Our return trip to the United States included the bonuses of a visit in Paris and an outing at Expo 58 in Brussels (the first World's Fair to be held since the end of World War II).

James Robinson's dream of linking the idealism of young Americans to the development of emerging African nations proves to have a lasting impact. During a visit from Crossroad Africa volunteers to the South Lawn of the White House in 1962, President John F. Kennedy publicly acknowledged that the imaginative program had played a major role in convincing him to establish the Peace Corps.

6

Equipping Myself for Ministry

S INCE I STILL INTENDED TO become a Presbyterian
pastor, it was time for me to focus my attention on a
seminary education. There had never been any question in my
mind about where I would acquire this training. I was headed
for Union Theological Seminary in New York City, the
alma mater of Jim Robinson, my Crossroads Africa mentor.
Further influencing my steps were three Berea professors who
had earned doctoral degrees at Union. (Two others had completed their studies at Yale Divinity School.)

My total exposure to higher education had consisted
of time spent at two rural institutions. By contrast, Union,
founded in 1836, stood at the peak of educational stature
and majesty. An imposing quadrangle of ornamented stone
in the English Gothic style, it occupied two city blocks of

Morningside Heights (and would later acquire additional property). Its tranquil, shaded courtyard offered shelter from the traffic noise of Broadway and the rumble of the IRT West Side subway line. The complex included dormitory rooms, professorial residences, offices, classrooms, a refectory, a handsomely furnished reception hall, and two chapels. Surrounding this magnificent citadel of theological reflection and inquiry were Columbia University, Teachers College, Barnard College, the Juilliard School of Music (which in later years relocated to Columbus Circle), Jewish Theological Seminary, and the imposing Riverside Church that had been commissioned and paid for by John D. Rockefeller, Jr.

A block distant from the seminary was the International House, a remarkable residence for hundreds of overseas students who came to New York City to further their education. It was a wonderful place to visit for meals, lectures, social occasions, and other special events and provided me with further exposure to an international ethos and new friendships.

When I arrived at Union, the Morningside Heights skyline was undergoing a dramatic change—construction of the 19-story Interchurch Center one block away from the seminary. Quickly acquiring the nickname of the "God Box,"

the modern structure was intended to be tangible evidence of growing ecumenical unity among Protestant denominations.

Groundbreaking ceremonies had taken place in 1957, and on October 12, 1958, U. S. President Dwight D. Eisenhower (himself a nominal Presbyterian) was the featured speaker at the laying of the cornerstone for this modern facility. Several hundred church dignitaries (including Eugene Carson Blake, former Stated Clerk of the United Presbyterian Church and then President of the National Council of Churches) and public officials paraded the short distance from Riverside Church to the construction site. For reasons still unknown to me, I was selected to be part of the procession and to carry a banner of my denomination. It was my first time in the presence of our country's chief executive. In later years the Interchurch Center (which opened in May 1960) was to become the home base for much of my professional career.

In those days, Union could lay claim with some justification to being the most distinguished—and the most liberal—Protestant seminary in the English-speaking world. Its faculty included some of the giants of American theology, headed by Reinhold Niebuhr, the prolific commentator on public affairs. This so-called Christian realist, author of *The Nature and Destiny of Man* in 1943, had been instrumental in bringing Paul Tillich to Union after that prominent theologian opposed the rise of Naziism and left Germany. Tillich's *The Courage to Be,* his seminal work about meaninglessness and anxiety, became a standard reading assignment throughout the world of higher education.

Another one of the academic stars on the faculty and one of my favorite professors was James Muilenburg, whose lectures and dramatic descriptions of the creation stories from the book of Genesis would annually fill the largest lecture hall on campus with rapt audiences. (Watching him assume the role of Adam discussing with God what to call the new animal with a long neck and no voice that God had created was to see the Bible come alive.)

I also was powerfully impressed by Robert McAfee Brown, a Presbyterian minister and powerful advocate for social, economic, and gender justice, and Robert Handy, a leading American church historian.

Given the strength of that faculty, it was no small wonder that some of the country's most prominent preachers, scholars, and church leaders, as well as organists and church musicians were alumni of the seminary and its School of Sacred Music.

Union may have been known for its liberal theology, but its enrollment policies were still racially cautious. When I registered, the seminary had only four Black students: Joseph Roberts (who then belonged to the African Methodist Episcopal Church); Robert Hood (who was preparing for the Anglican priesthood); Jim Forbes (raised in the Holiness tradition), and me. In later life, after service as a Presbyterian minister and denomination executive, Roberts would become the senior pastor of Ebenezer Baptist Church (Martin Luther King, Jr.'s congregation in Atlanta), and Forbes would be named senior pastor of Riverside Church. Hood's final post before dying at a relatively young age was as Director of the Center for African American Studies at Adelphi University in New York.

My first roommate in Hastings Hall was Charles Conrad Hoover, who also was preparing to become a Presbyterian minister. After graduating from Union, though, he earned a doctorate in ministry from The Catholic University of America. Conrad eventually converted to Catholicism and was ordained to the priesthood.

During this period, I underwent an identity transformation of sorts. I had originally been christened "James" after a favorite uncle. My middle name came from a paternal grandfather, and my family always called me "Oscar." Upon reaching Union, I changed my signature from "James O. McCloud"

to "J. Oscar McCloud." That shift was prompted in large measure by the receptionist at the switchboard in Hastings Hall who frequently called me "Jim." I determined that he was confusing me with Jim Forbes (Don't we all look alike?), so I decided to drop "James" and use the initial "J." Over the years, when asked what it stands for, I have enjoyed telling unsuspecting persons that it is shorthand for "Geronimo" leaving them to ponder whether that name begins with a "J" or a "G."

My matriculation at Union also meant that I was registered as a student at Auburn Theological Seminary. That Presbyterian institution which had been established in 1818 to prepare ministers for the American frontier was one of the first seminaries in the country to admit African Americans, Asians, and women. Financially weakened by the Great Depression, it had relocated to the Union campus in 1939, while retaining its denominational affiliation and autonomy. (Several years ago it moved its facilities from the Union campus to the nearby Interchurch Center.)

All candidates for the ministry at Union were required to perform at least one year of service referred to as "field work" at a church or other not-for-profit organization. My initial assignment was to the Willis Avenue United Methodist Church. That congregation could date its origins back to 1869 when it had been established as the First United Methodist Church of North New York at the corner of 141st Street and Willis Avenue. Its massive stone sanctuary contained a Moeller pipe organ, and the education building was large enough to include a full-size gymnasium.

However, the church had fallen on hard times as that section of the Bronx deteriorated badly. It occupied a dirty, drug-infested, crime-ridden neighborhood of public housing and neglected slums—a virtual catalog of urban dysfunction. Church membership had dropped precipitously. Many of the white members had left the Bronx; most of the new members were African American, and the church budget could no longer support building maintenance or program expenses.

I chose to work at that institution because of its relative proximity to the seminary and the availability of public transportation. Every Wednesday afternoon and Sunday morning during the school year I would climb aboard a city bus that would transport me across Harlem and over the Willis

Avenue Bridge into the South Bronx and drop me off in front of the church.

My job description encompassed teaching Sunday school and leading other youth activities. I expanded that assignment to include taking the young people of the congregation on Saturday field trips. It was a way to expose them to artistic and cultural venues in Manhattan and elsewhere that they might otherwise never have experienced.

When the young pastor who had hired me died, I suddenly was the only program staff person on the payroll. A somewhat desperate District Superintendent of the denomination needed to find a ministerial replacement. Forsaking any allegiance to Methodist church polity, he begged me to remain. Thus it was that this non-ordained Presbyterian with only a smattering of theological education found himself preaching regularly from a Methodist pulpit and helping to administer the sacraments. At the request of John Carrington, the new pastor who was appointed the next spring, I continued my work in the Bronx during the next two academic years at Union.

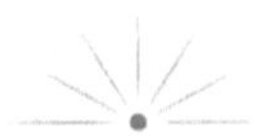

However, my life involved more than study and work. When time and finances permitted, I enjoyed taking advantage of shows at the famous Apollo Theatre. Its marquee stretched above the 125th Street sidewalk in the heart of Harlem and colorfully advertised current and coming attractions. This citadel of Black performance by famous artists was within a few city blocks of the seminary, and I was able to enjoy the talented offerings of musicians like Count Basie, Louis Armstrong, Ella Fitzgerald, and other giants of the jazz and pop music world.

Interruptions of my field work included a stint during the summer of 1959 when I directed a recreation program for young people from the historic Gillespie Selden Institute in Cordele, Georgia. This Black boarding school, like Boggs Academy, was founded by Presbyterians at the beginning of the 20th century to educate and train African American young people for a variety of professions. The next summer I lived in New York and commuted regularly to Philadelphia. There I learned how to read census tracts and prepare data for analysis after the local presbytery hired me to conduct a survey of South Philadelphia's African American population.

However, before I encountered those experiences, broader and deeper developments in American society began to change the direction of my life at the seminary. On February 1, 1960, a small group of students from A & T University, a historically Black institution in Greensboro, North Carolina, staged its now-famous sit-in at the local Woolworth's lunch counter. This protest of the store's refusal to serve African Americans soon was replicated throughout the South and, indeed, around the country.

Ella Baker, an alumna of Shaw University in Raleigh (another Black college) and Executive Director of the Southern Christian Leadership Conference in Atlanta, correctly sensed a pivotal moment in the history of race relations. She invited students from other Black colleges around the South to meet at Shaw during Easter weekend that spring. More than one hundred undergraduates, including some who would become legends in the coming civil rights struggle, assembled and formed the Student Nonviolent Coordinating Committee (SNCC)—or, as it came to be called: Snick.

Even as these events were unfolding, I joined several of my fellow Union students to form the Student Interracial Ministry (SIM). We mobilized and joined picket lines around the Woolworth establishments in Times Square and at 116th Street and Broadway (where I heard myself called a Communist by an onlooker for the first time). However, our principal strategy to promote better race relations was to place African American seminarians as assistant pastors on the staff of white churches and to arrange for white seminary students to serve Black congregations. In the original group of placements were my Union classmates, John Collins from the United Methodist Church, Charles Helms, a Presbyterian from the South, Conrad Hoover, my first roommate, and Jim Forbes.

After graduating from Lane College in 1960, Robbie visited me in New York. The chance to end our lengthy separation from each other convinced us that we wanted to get married. Since we didn't have the financial resources to pay for a formal wedding ceremony, we decided to elope. As Billy Edd Wheeler, my song-writing fellow alumnus from Warren Wilson Junior College put it, "We got married in a fever/ Hotter than a pepper sprout."

Robbie had secured a position as a high school social studies teacher in Ashburn, Georgia, the municipal center of Turner County in the lower part of Georgia. I joined her there as soon as my summer obligations were completed. The Rev. Millard F. Adams, pastor of the small C. K. Smith Memorial Presbyterian Church in Albany, Georgia, presided over our marriage on September 13, 1960, in the living room of his manse. His wife and a church member witnessed the simple ceremony. During the wedding I presented Robbie with an "imperfect" diamond ring and the promise—one that she declined to accept—to buy her a perfect gem sometime in the future.

Our honeymoon lasted only a few days. Had we not been deeply involved in our attention to each other, we might have been more aware of the emerging challenges to racial segregation that were in progress all around us and would soon be known as the Albany Movement. Then Robbie prepared to begin her teaching career, and I returned to New York.

There I remembered (or perhaps discovered) that scholarship students were required to obtain permission from the seminary before getting married. I nervously secured an appointment with Bob Lynn, who had just been named Dean of Auburn Seminary. Seated in his office, I described my lengthy relationship with Robbie, told him about our recent wedding, and assured him that I wanted to keep our marriage a secret. He quietly assured me that it would not become a subject of public knowledge and that my financial support was safe.

An academic high point of my return to Union came when I was able to attend presentations by Alan Paton, a guest lecturer at the seminary. The acclaimed South African author of *Cry the Beloved Country* and *Too Late the Phalarope* gave me a new and deeper perception about life in South Africa—an understanding that intensified my desire to learn more. It also helped me to compose a term paper about the differing forms of racial discrimination in the United States and South Africa for a class taught by Reinhold Niebuhr. (I still am inordinately proud that the paper earned me a B+ grade from Dr. Niebuhr.)

The rest of that year until my graduation in the spring of 1961 was happily marked by periodic short visits from my secret new bride. Then came the beautiful evening commencement ceremony in the magnificent sanctuary of Riverside Church. It was one of those "I can't believe this is happening to me" events. Robbie could not attend, but my mother was there—just barely. She had flown from Georgia to be part of the occasion and was staying with a friend in the Bronx. My brother, Elijah, who then lived in Brooklyn, was late picking her up and bringing her to the service.

7

Ordained and Called

URING MY TIME IN SEMINARY I was what Presbyterians describe as "under the care of" Knox-Hodge Presbytery. That regional governing body was composed of a small number of African American pastors and Ruling Elders who met only three times each year. At their June 14, 1961 gathering, in a simple weekday ceremony at the church on the Boggs Academy campus, I was ordained as an "evangelist." (This step was in accordance with a provision in the *Book of Order* for validating ministerial candidates who had not yet received a call.)

Davie Street Presbyterian Church in Raleigh, North Carolina was a well-established Black congregation that had been in existence since the 1870s. As I will later describe, I did eventually receive a call to become its pastor. However, the route to that destination was circuitous. It involved a series of missteps and misunderstandings that could easily have short-circuited the entire process.

The confusion began midway through my senior year at Union when the Davie Street session invited me to preach. In those days, an offer of that kind virtually assured one of being called as a church's new pastor. However, a month before my scheduled appearance in that congregation's pulpit, a letter from the church withdrew the invitation. The message that I received cited the high cost of my travel as the reason for the cancellation. In my response I was quick to express anger and disappointment. I further vowed to myself that I would never set foot in the Davie Street Presbyterian Church.

Even as I was engaged in this correspondence, though, I also had submitted an application for a position in the Student Interracial Ministry program. As chance would have it, another congregation in Raleigh—the historically white and progressive United Church of Christ—invited me to a summer internship. I quickly accepted its offer.

My mother and wife attended the ordination service on the Boggs campus. Afterwards, Robbie and I, with the assistance of my brother, Willie, purchased a used Plymouth and rented a trailer in Waynesboro. From there we drove to Bremen where we picked up some of Robbie's belongings and continued to Raleigh.

Perhaps our grandest wedding present was the discovery that a member of the United Church had arranged for us to occupy her home while she spent the summer in New York City. Dr. Susanne Freund, a professor at nearby Meredith College, requested only that we care for her cocker spaniel while she was away. The lovely house was in an all-white section of town, however, our hostess became a dear friend who later participated in a member exchange program between the United Church and the Davie Street congregation. (Many years later, at Dr. Freund's request, I participated in her funeral service.)

That summer I assisted the pastor, Colin Kilburn, in all aspects of his ministry, including involvement with the African American Citizens Association and the Raleigh chapter of the NAACP. During that work I also came to know Don Shriver, Associate Pastor of the West Raleigh Presbyterian Church. Don would go on to become a professor of religion and campus minister at North Carolina State University, later a professor of ethics at Emory University, and then President of Union Theological Seminary, my alma mater. At any rate, I was sufficiently active in church and community affairs to be recognized in a steadily widening circle of leaders.

One of the ecclesiastical oddities of Raleigh was that it had a white First Baptist Church and a Black church of the same name. Their shared origin was as a bi-racial congregation before the Civil War. The reasons for their division are varied and unclear, but their sanctuaries still stand on opposite sides of the state capitol building, and they do find ways to collaborate.

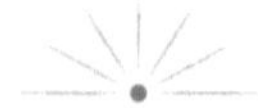

Later that summer, while my senior pastor was on vacation, I received a call from Clarence Lightner, a member of the Session at the Davie Street Presbyterian Church. He was a prominent funeral director who in later years would be elected as the city's first Black mayor. We had met several times at community leadership gatherings. His church's Men's Day speaker was ill and had been forced to cancel his appearance. Lightner was hoping that I would accept an invitation to take that person's place. I was still annoyed by my previous contact with his congregation, so I declined his persistent requests several times (without explaining my reason). However, I finally agreed to accept the offer.

My presentation must have been well received. As I later learned, immediately after my speech to the Men's Day event, the church's Session set in motion the steps needed to extend me a call to become its pastor.

The timing was good for everyone involved. The congregation, which had called—and lost—a string of short-tenured ministers, was again without a pastor, and I was going to be without a job at the end of the summer. We began negotiations, and by the end of August 1961, I received a call.

Jim Costen delivered the homily at my installation service. He and I had met through our churches' shared membership in the small, all-Black Cape Fear Presbytery.

Born in Omaha, Nebraska, he had been raised as a Roman Catholic. However, he became a United Presbyterian minister while attending Johnson C. Smith University and Seminary and then was one of the first African Americans to earn a theology degree at Wake Forest University.

When I met him, he was the pastor of Mt. Pisgah Presbyterian Church in Rocky Mount, North Carolina. He and his wife, Melva, had successfully fought for the racial integration of the school to which they sent their youngest child. They also helped to arrange the November 27, 1962 visit to their city by Martin Luther King, Jr. King spoke to a large audience at Booker T. Washington High School that included Mahala Jackson, the renowned gospel singer.

What distinguished Dr. King's remarks that day was that he used the "I have a dream" refrain and other rhetorical turns of phrase that he would employ in his powerful speech at the March on Washington the next year.

Although more than two years had passed since the initial Greensboro sit-ins, protests were still alive and well throughout North Carolina and its capital city. Students and other Raleigh citizens continued their demonstrations against the city's segregated businesses and facilities. One of the targets identified by students from two of the historically Black colleges (Shaw and St. Augustine) was the downtown S & W Cafeteria on Fayetteville Street.

Despite being a newly installed pastor at the Davie Street church, I felt an obligation to support the students. Charles Ward, pastor of the Black First Baptist Church, and I selected a day on which to position ourselves at the head of the customer line for the S & W lunchtime serving. A restaurant employee blocked our forward movement, and we stepped aside only to permit white customers to enter. When it became clear that we were not going to be served nor arrested, we left the premises.

After I returned home and reported to my pregnant wife what I had tried to do, she was furious. Robbie let me know in no uncertain terms that she was not in favor of me having risked going to jail while she was preparing to give birth to our first child. Apparently, the battle for justice could have domestic consequences.

Another business targeted for action by the protestors was a Howard Johnson motel just outside the city. Making it an especially attractive target for a publicized protest was the fact that it was owned by Luther Hodges, a former North Carolina governor and current member of President John F. Kennedy's cabinet.

Picketing was scheduled for a Sunday following worship, and we pastors who had participated with the students in the planning of the protest promised to encourage our members to join us. Given the traditional conservatism of my congregation's lay leadership, I was pleasantly surprised when a significant number of them joined the demonstration.

A third civil rights confrontation with which I became publicly associated involved student demonstrations at the segregated Ambassador Theatre. William Enloe, Mayor of Raleigh (who also happened to be a member of First Presbyterian Church) was the district manager of several movie houses, including the Ambassador. Although perceived as moderate by his white constituents, he resisted the idea of integrating the movie houses and threatened to resign his position as mayor.

Because of my association with the students, I found myself attracting attention from the local press. However, that publicity didn't seem to harm my acceptance by the students or other Raleigh citizens. Indeed, it was during this period that I also began receiving inquiries from Black Presbyterian churches around the country who wanted to consider me as a candidate for their pulpits. Clearly, my pastorate with the Davie Street congregation was helping to shape my leadership skill and to shed some of my tendencies to be impatient.

From its earliest days in North America, the Presbyterian church in all its forms had been plagued by the same racism that infected the rest of the New World. However, as the civil rights momentum of the Sixties gained strength, an old reality became clear: neither prayers nor proclamations by the Church would bring about visibility and power for people of color. Black Presbyterians themselves would have to be the instruments of change.

That struggle had been going on at least since the 1893 organization of the Afro Presbyterian Council. In 1947 the group changed its name to the Council of the North and West, and by 1964 it had evolved into Concerned Presbyterians United, a group of Black ministers that I helped to form and joined.

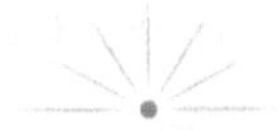

One of the most influential members of that organization was Gayraud Wilmore, a fierce advocate of racial justice. A native of Philadelphia, "Gay" had been a member of a combat unit of the 92nd Infantry (the "Buffalo Soldiers") in Italy during World War II. He was also a graduate of both Lincoln University, the country's oldest historically Black college, and its related Lincoln Seminary. While serving churches as a pastor in the Philadelphia area, Wilmore worked to desegregate the public schools in West Chester, and in 1951 his son was the first Black student to attend an all-white elementary school.

In 1953 he further focused his work on behalf of civil rights after becoming the associate executive of the United Presbyterian Church, U.S.A's Department of Social Education and Action. He then joined the faculty of Pittsburgh Theological Seminary as a professor of social ethics and the only Black faculty member until 1963.

That spring my denomination's General Assembly, meeting in Des Moines, Iowa, took the most dramatic organizational step in its history. After a similar action by the National Council of Churches, it established the Commission on Religion and Race and named Wilmore as its Executive Director. The Commission's assignment was to function as the focal point for race relations and to coordinate efforts between Presbyterians and other interfaith groups. That assignment included marshaling the denomination's response and participation in civil rights protests and marches.

The Iowa General Assembly is also remembered for its election of a Moderator by the closest vote in the denomination's history. The two finalists were Herman Turner, the politically moderate white pastor of Covenant Presbyterian Church in Atlanta, and Edler Hawkins, the African American pastor of St. Augustine Presbyterian Church in the Bronx, New York. Each had served his congregation for three decades. When the voting of the delegates yielded a tie, Hawkins supported his white opponent. At the next year's General Assembly in Oklahoma (which I attended), Hawkins was almost unanimously elected as the first Black moderator in the denomination's history.

Elsewhere in the country the protests against racial segregation were escalating. In Birmingham, Alabama, Dr. King arrived to lead the opposition, and the authorities' response with water cannons and police dogs was widely televised.

It became broadly understood that A. Philip Randolph and Bayard Rustin were organizing a massive demonstration in the nation's capital. Soon it was common knowledge that the March on Washington for Jobs and Freedom would take place on August 28, 1963, and that large crowds were expected. In Raleigh, as elsewhere around the country, Black Americans and individuals who were sympathetic to their cause conducted fundraising appeals, chartered buses and made other travel arrangements to get themselves to the nation's capital that day. I had every intention of joining the march and was pleased that members of my normally cautious and even conservative congregation had caught the spirit of the occasion and planned to travel with me.

It was not my first march in Washington. In 1959, during my first year at seminary, Mr. Randolph had organized a demonstration in the capital for jobs and desegregated schools to which I had led a church youth group. But this venture dwarfed that worthwhile but modest effort.

Robbie suppressed any anxiety she might have harbored about the dangers that might accompany the march and instead encouraged me to participate. Knowing that I had her support helped to make the six-hour ride to the nation's capital exciting and inspirational.

However, even the positive emotions during that trip to the nation's capital could not begin to trigger the same kind of powerful feelings that swept through me when I stepped off the bus in Washington and saw tens of thousands of people filling the Mall in front of the Lincoln Memorial.

I realized immediately that I would not be able to get any closer to the rostrum, so I found a spot of shade beneath a tree and turned my pocket radio to the program speakers. I may not have been able to express my feelings in words that day, but somehow, as I listened to the speeches and especially the climactic exhortations of Dr. King, I knew that the rest of my life would be focused on the campaign for racial and economic justice. This goal would be a part of my ministry because I wanted a better life for my children and future generations.

On November 18, 1963, Robbie gave birth to Ann Michelle McCloud in Raleigh's Wake Memorial Hospital. (Part of the excitement about her arrival was overshadowed a few days later by the assassination of President Kennedy.) She was baptized by Jim Costen during a service in the Davie Street Presbyterian Church. Although she received the first name of Robbie's closest friend, we quickly became accustomed to using her middle name—that of my French tutor at Berea College. Ever since encountering it for the first time, I found "Michelle" to be the most beautiful female name I had ever heard.

Joseph Metz Rollins, who was field director of our denomination's Board of Christian Education, came to Raleigh in 1964 to recruit me as his successor. "Metz" was based in Nashville, where he also was Vice President of a branch of Dr. Martin Luther King, Jr.'s Southern Christian Leadership

Conference and a Director of the National Committee of Black Churchmen, an organization dedicated to advocating for racial awareness within churches.

Since I was experiencing a steadily growing desire to be involved in the work of race relations, I felt deeply honored by the invitation and accepted with little hesitation. My job description, in essence, was to be another set of eyes and ears of our denomination throughout the South. Because my work would involve a lot of travel, and since Atlanta was the hub for an expanding network of air routes, I chose to locate my office in that city.

Robbie was particularly pleased to be leaving North Carolina and returning to her native state. During the time we lived in Raleigh, she often did not feel warmly welcomed by many of the people she encountered, including some of the members in the Davie Street Presbyterian Church. Nonetheless, she anticipated—correctly—that the social scene of Atlanta, which was becoming rapidly urbanized, would be more hospitable than the small-town patterns of life in the North Carolina capital.

We began making plans for our departure.

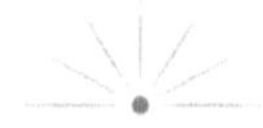

Although our tenure in Raleigh was relatively brief, it was there that I began to develop pastoral and leadership skills.

Years later when I was invited to return to the Davie Street church to speak at its 155th anniversary, the title of my message was "Abounding in Hope," and I expressed my appreciation for the church's support of a once-inexperienced pastor.

Oscar McCloud officiating an infant baptism at Fifth Avenue Presbyterian in Manhattan in 2010.

(From right) Henry Pruitt, fishing guide, Eugene Turner, and Oscar McCloud on a fishing trip for sockeye salmon in the Kenai Peninsula in southern Alaska.

(From right) Oscar McCloud; Pauline Webb, part of the central committee of the World Council of Churches (WCC); Winnie Mandela; staff member of the WCC; Nelson Mandela, and staff member of the WCC.

A joint worship service of the United Church and First Congregational Church in Raleigh, North Carolina, in the summer of 1961. (From right) Oscar McCloud; Collins Kilburn, pastor of the United Church; Howard Cunningham, pastor of First Congregational Church; Mary Kilburn, spouse of Collins Kilburn; Robbie McCloud, spouse of Oscar McCloud; and Mrs. Cunningham, spouse of Rev. Cunningham. At the time of the service, Oscar was a student interracial ministry intern at The United Church.

The McCloud family home where Oscar was born. The photo was taken in the 1980s, fifty years after Oscar's birth in 1936.

(From right) Oscar's late wife Robbie McCloud, as well as his daughters Michelle and Cassandra.

Oscar and his wife Kathy on their wedding day in St. Petersburg, Florida, on May 26, 2012.

The McCloud extended family at the 50th wedding anniversary of Oscar's parents in 1977.

(From right) Oscar McCloud; Gayraud Wilmore, Executive Director of the Council on Church and Race; Sophia LaRusso, staff member of the Council on Church and Race (United Presbyterian Church in the United States of America).

Oscar meeting with Bishop of Johannesburg Desmond Tutu in Harare, Zimbabwe, in 1985. McCloud, along with 100 other church leaders from the World Council of Churches, met in an emergency meeting to discuss the situation in South Africa.

Oscar with a fifty-four-pound king salmon while fishing in Alaska in 2002.

Oscar's election as General Director of the Program Agency in 1973 at the General Assembly of the Presbyterian Church (USA). (From right), Robbie McCloud; Oscar McCloud; Mary Jane Patterson, director of the Washington office of the UPCUSA; and John Evans, executive of the Presbyterian Church (USA).

Eighteen-year-old Oscar on a tobacco farm in Windsor, Connecticut, in 1954.

The one-room schoolhouse in Waynesboro, Georgia, where Oscar attended primary school. The school served seven grades and Oscar walked two miles to and from school every day. It was the only public education available to Black, elementary children.

8

At the Heart of
the Movement

OUR ARRIVAL IN ATLANTA FOLLOWED on the heels of a racial brouhaha that had attracted international attention. It began in December 1962, when Clinton Warner, an activist Black physician, purchased a home in Peyton Forest—a subdivision of the formerly all-white section of the city known as Cascade Heights. Mayor Ivan Allen's first response was to order the erection of a concrete barricade across the road leading into that part of town to discourage further incursion by African Americans.

It was a move that temporarily weakened Atlanta's claim of being the city "too busy to hate." Quickly labeled as "Atlanta's Berlin Wall" in news stories around the world, the blockade had a short lifespan. It was quickly ruled unconstitutional by the courts, and white residents soon were rapidly selling their properties to a wave of Black citizens ready to move into the formerly segregated area.

Robbie and I rented an apartment off Simpson Road for a short while but then purchased a 1.8-acre property with its own virtual forest of pine trees beside Peyton Road. We also joined SWAP (Southwest Atlantans for Progress), a community group that tried to maintain a racially balanced neighborhood. That venture was short-lived; almost all of the remaining white families sold their homes and left the neighborhood, and the southwest quadrant of the city was soon a predominantly middle-to-upper-class African American section.

We were especially pleased when the new arrivals to our part of town included Jim and Melva Costen, our friends from North Carolina. Jim had received a call to become the founding pastor of Church of the Master, a new and intentionally bi-racial congregation on the west side of the city. Our family affiliated itself with that church, and we and the Costens, who lived close to our home, enjoyed many opportunities to socialize with each other. (The menus at our shared meals and backyard cookouts often included produce from the large garden that I planted.)

Atlanta was rapidly establishing itself as a major city. Among the factors that were spurring its influence and prominence were the presence of the Atlanta University Center (the unique federation of historically Black Atlanta University, Clark, Morehouse, Morris Brown, and Spelman Colleges, and the Interdenominational Theological Center). The strong leadership and alumni of these institutions provided a good balance to the relatively moderate racial attitudes of the city's white business and political leadership.

As a result, signs of growth and a new cosmopolitan attitude were everywhere. The Playboy Club opened for business in 1965; the Braves baseball team relocated from Milwaukee to a hastily constructed stadium in 1966; the Hyatt Regency Hotel with its dramatic open atrium began to attract crowds in 1967. Interstate highways were blasting their way through the center of the city.

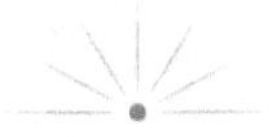

According to my official job description, I was now "on the staff of the Board of Christian Education of the United Presbyterian Church, U.S.A." My new position in Atlanta called for me to represent the denomination as field representative in a 17-state section of the country (i.e., the area that the U.S. Census Bureau considered to be "The South"). As such I was responsible for "dealing with problems and issues arising from the struggle for equal rights for all Americans and the movement for desegregation of schools, churches, and places of public accommodation." The delineation of my responsibilities further stated that I offered "specialized information, guidance, and practical help to ministers, churches, presbyteries, synods, and other groups and individuals involved in the racial crisis." (Whew!)

If that mandate were not sufficiently inclusive—and impossible to fulfill—I also was unofficially available to assist Gay Wilmore at the new Commission on Religion and Race. Since his unit had limited funds and staff, he was empowered to draft the assistance of any organization and its personnel within the denomination.

It was exciting to be living and working in the city that was the virtual headquarters of the civil rights movement. In addition to being the home base for the Southern Christian Leadership Conference, the Student Nonviolent Coordinating Committee, and the Southern Regional Council, it also housed regional offices for, among other organizations, the National Urban League, the Congress of Racial Equality (CORE), the ACLU, the American Jewish Committee, the AFL-CIO Civil Rights Division, the Episcopal Church Society for Racial Unity, and the American Friends Service Committee. All of their representatives were, in effect, my colleagues in the struggle for equal rights and justice, and we all were in frequent contact, both formal and informal, with each other—often for lunch in the by-then-desegregated restaurants of downtown Atlanta.

Among my favorite co-workers was Frances Pauley, the longtime and politically astute Executive Director of the Georgia Council on Human Relations. It was through her recommendation that I became a member of the Georgia Advisory Committee to the U.S. Civil Rights Commission. Another close colleague was Herman Sweatt, her Assistant Director, who also taught classes at Atlanta University. Sweatt already was a noted historical figure in civil rights circles, having been part of the legal suit (*Sweatt v. Painter*) that had led to the integration of the University of Texas Law School in 1950. And then there was the remarkable Connie Curry, on the field staff for the American Friends Service Committee Agnes Scott College graduate and civil rights activist in Mississippi who became the first white woman to serve on the SNCC executive committee.

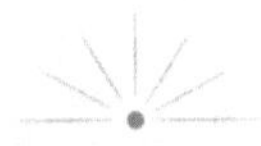

Since one person clearly could not perform all the duties outlined by my denomination, I soon attached myself to the Georgia Advisory Committee of the U.S. Civil Rights Commission. One of my first assignments from that organization was to test compliance with the Civil Rights Act of 1964, which President Lyndon Johnson had recently signed into law. I did so by making reservations for my family at the Holiday Inns in Brunswick and Waycross, Georgia, and then driving down to the southeastern corner of the state to learn whether those bookings would be honored. (In these situations, I did not identify my affiliation.)

The motels accepted my reservations—after a fashion. When I told a local Black pastor about my room number at the Brunswick facility, he explained that it was "reserved" for African American guests. As he further described, Senator Leroy Johnson, Georgia's first Black legislator since the Civil War, had been assigned to stay in the same space.

In Waycross, I was offered space that adjoined a noisy laundry room that was subject to flooding. In both cases, the hotel clerks only reluctantly honored my requests to be booked into better quarters.

Soon after settling in Atlanta, Robbie and I became increasingly aware that Michelle was subject to physical seizures. When we had her tested for allergies, she reacted negatively to almost every food group. Robbie one day declared with exasperation, "I don't know how I'm going to keep this baby alive." I still remember driving all over Atlanta in search of the goat milk that Michelle's digestive system could tolerate and finally discovering that the concentrated soy milk available at a neighborhood pharmacy was a suitable substitute. The only animal flesh to which Michelle was not allergic was lamb, and for many years, it was she who consumed all of that expensive meat which came into our house.

It also became obvious that other facets of her development did not seem normal. Consequently, we were saddened but not completely surprised when her physicians diagnosed her as developmentally delayed. We knew then that Michelle would be classified as someone with a permanent disability and began to plan accordingly for her future care. Central to our decision-making, however, was our determination that she would remain with us in our home for as long as possible.

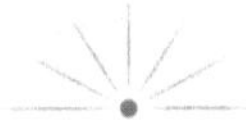

My work was seldom on the front line of the anti-racist protests that swirled around the region. However, I always was conscious of being in a still-dangerous region. The 16th Street Baptist Church in Birmingham had been bombed by Ku Klux Klan members soon after the March on Washington. During the summer that we left Raleigh, three civil rights workers had been killed in Philadelphia, Mississippi.

However, I had the opportunity to form friendships with an assortment of colorful leaders and to arrange my own travel schedule.

I wore many "hats" during those Atlanta years. They included presiding over the meetings of a community support group for State Representative Julian Bond when the Georgia General Assembly refused to seat him because of his opposition to U.S. foreign policy. (By sheer coincidence, Julian's sister, Jane, became the first secretary I hired in Atlanta.)

I remember with delight a meeting with Dr. King and other SCLC leaders that was interrupted by Hosea Williams who loudly and angrily criticized a colleague. Dr. King smilingly responded to the outburst by reminding Williams of Jesus' admonition to forgive wrongdoers "seven times seven." (Williams, incidentally, had been raised in the Butler Memorial Presbyterian Church in Savannah—a background that perhaps influenced the decision of the United Presbyterian Church to underwrite a portion of his salary.)

For a time, I also served as Vice Moderator with Andrew Young of the Child Development Group of Mississippi that managed funds for a statewide Head Start program.

On the evening of March 7, 1965, like many Americans, I was watching a television showing of the film *Judgment at Nuremberg*. The broadcast was interrupted by a live newscast that showed Alabama state troopers and other law enforcement officers viciously attacking a procession of about five hundred civil rights protestors. The demonstrators, led by John Lewis and Hosea Williams, were attempting to cross the Edmund Pettus Bridge in Selma, Alabama, as the beginning of a march to Montgomery. It was a bloody and disturbing scene as the state officials, some of them with police dogs, wielded clubs, whips, and tear gas to halt the marchers.

I immediately prepared to leave for Selma, even as Martin King issued a call for supporters of civil rights to come to Alabama. By Tuesday, March 9, I had joined a crowd of more than two thousand marchers, led by King and other SCLC figures, who had gathered at the Brown Chapel AME Church and set off toward the Pettus Bridge. When we were met by armed and angry police, King halted the march, led our crowd in prayer, and guided us away from the bridge. I will confess to a deep sense of relief when the march was halted and further violence averted.

From Atlanta, to which I returned, I followed the continuing events as the federal government intervened directly to protect the marchers who resumed their progress and arrived in the Alabama state capital some two weeks later.

There were other demonstrations that I observed—some small, some large. The attempt to register Black voters in Hattiesburg, Mississippi, was the culmination of several years of work by SNCC workers. What I remember about that event was flying to Jackson and renting a car to drive to Hattiesburg. The agency gave me a sporty Buick Wildcat—further confirming my suspicion that the rental offices intentionally leased highly recognizable vehicles to individuals like me to make us easier target for possible harassment or aggression. (I exchanged it for a less conspicuous car before continuing my way.)

As described in the *Mississippi Encyclopedia*, the Hattiesburg "campaign" was evidence of growing support for the civil rights movement by church leaders. Strongly promoted by the Council on Church and Race, several dozen Northern Presbyterian pastors joined by Episcopalian, Methodist, and Disciples of Christ ministers, as well as Unitarian leaders and Jewish rabbis, had marched to demand voting rights for local African Americans. Nine Presbyterian clergy were arrested and each fined $200 and sentenced to four months in jail.

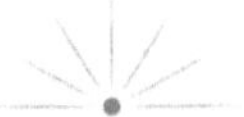

One of the most memorable events I witnessed took place during the spring of 1966. James Meredith, a Mississippi native and Army veteran, had integrated the University of Mississippi in 1962 with the support of federal troops, and then went on to graduate from that institution. On June 5, 1966, equipped with only a helmet and a walking stick, he began what he described as a "March Against Fear"—a 220-mile trek on foot from Memphis, Tennessee, to Jackson, Mississippi. His stated intent was to encourage African Americans in Mississippi to register to vote and to challenge the culture of fear perpetuated by white supremacists in the state.

Meredith crossed the Mississippi border on the morning of June 6, 1966, accompanied by a handful of friends and supporters. State police and FBI agents monitored the march while reporters and photographers trailed behind. However, his solo exercise took on national dimensions on the second day when he was wounded by a white man who fired a shotgun at him, requiring Meredith's hospitalization. Led by Dr. King, Stokely Carmichael (the recently elected chairman of SNCC) and James Farmer and Floyd McKissick from CORE (Congress of Racial Equality), film stars, many other public figures, and thousands of additional supporters poured into the area to join the line of march. Within hours, SCLC, SNCC, and CORE vowed to continue Meredith's pilgrimage.

I caught a flight to Jackson and joined the marchers about 20 miles north of the city. After walking for several hours and perhaps 10 miles, we arrived at the campus of Tougaloo College, a historically Black institution. There the marchers were able to refresh themselves and listen to speeches by the march leaders. Perhaps the most dramatic development of the three-week event was Stokely Carmichael's declaration that racial segregation would now be met by "Black Power."

I myself did little marching, but there was one memorable exception. In 1967, Georgia's segregationist Governor Lester Maddox invited Governor Lurleen Wallace of Alabama and her husband, George, to speak to the Georgia Assembly. On that occasion, wearing my clerical collar and carrying an American flag (the only time in my life that I did so), I joined an interfaith group of ministers and university students who marched around the capital building to protest the presence of the Wallaces.

Given the seriousness and even danger of the times, it now seems surprising to remember that our time in Atlanta was a period when the McClouds and the Costens shared some thoroughly enjoyable experiences. We vacationed together (even visiting Hawaii on one occasion and taking a Caribbean cruise on another). Jim and I also drove with our wives from Atlanta to a conference at Ghost Ranch, the Presbyterian center in New Mexico, and then continued to a visit in his hometown of Omaha.

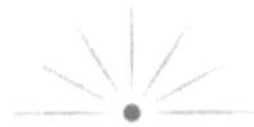

As the summer of 1965 drew to an end and Labor Day approached, it became clear that Robbie would soon be giving birth to our second child. It also seemed certain that she would need help with caring for Michelle. My mother was willing to assist, so we decided that I would drive to her home and bring her back to Atlanta with me. Jim Costen offered to keep me company on the trip. Because he and I left late in the day, we planned to spend the night in Waynesboro and return to Atlanta the next morning

Before leaving Waynesboro I called home and reached Robbie's mother, Inez Foster, who had come to Atlanta to be with her daughter. She greeted me with the announcement that I was the father of a new healthy daughter and informed me that Cassandra Anita McCloud had been born in St. Joseph's Hospital at three o'clock that morning. I was overcome with mixed emotions: happy that the birth had gone well, but disappointed that I wasn't with Robbie when it happened. Our second daughter was subsequently baptized by Jim Costen at the Church of the Master.

Meanwhile, Jim's career path was taking him in a new direction. When Johnson C. Smith Seminary's financial difficulties threatened the institution with closure, he led the effort to keep it open, become its dean, secure new students and finances, and align it with the historically Black Interdenominational Theological Center (ITC) in Atlanta. (He subsequently became the President of the new Presbyterian seminary and then of the ITC.)

Nearly a decade had elapsed since my trip to Liberia during the summer of 1958, and I had lost touch with most of the Crossroads Africa staff or alumni I had known. Consequently, I was pleasantly surprised when I was recruited to lead a summer work group to Ghana for six weeks during the summer of 1967.

The project that we were given closely resembled my first experience in Africa. Our assignment was the construction of a one-room schoolhouse in a village near a teacher training college.

Our group had been warmly welcomed when we Crossroaders arrived in Liberia ten years earlier. However, that greeting paled in comparison with the ceremonies arranged by the Ghanians. Treating us like celebrities, they staged a parade with music and dancing and presented us with gifts of food that included a live chicken.

Not all of my travels with Jim Costen were marked by innocent pleasure. For example, we had an especially challenging trip as we returned home from an SCLC meeting in Birmingham, Alabama. We had crossed the state line into Georgia on Route 78 and were passing through Bremen, Georgia. Jim was behind the wheel of his blue Oldsmobile 88, and he was driving too fast.

A Black man steering a large, shiny new General Motors vehicle with a license plate that identified its place of origin as Atlanta and traveling in excess of the speed limit was simply too tempting a catch for a white, small-town Georgia policeman to ignore. He pulled us over, asked to see Jim's car registration and driver's license, and informed him that he was speeding. When Jim disagreed, the officer ordered Jim to drive us to the police station in Bremen. There he ordered Jim out of his car and placed him under arrest.

Jim sometimes forgot that he no longer could employ the freedom of speech he enjoyed in his Nebraska birthplace; he had not stopped loudly protesting his innocence since we were first pulled over. The arresting officer's response was to lock Jim in a large cage-like enclosure with thick wooden bars at the back of a room in the police station. Jim noisily objected while repeatedly calling, "Oz, get me out of here."

I don't recall all the details of Jim's release. However, I do remember that producing my AAA membership card for the bond and handing over sufficient cash to pay the fine got us back on our way to Atlanta—with me driving. The situation in which we had found ourselves had the potential to be dangerous, but now that it was behind us, we were able to laugh—albeit a bit nervously.

Dr. Martin Luther King, Jr. was murdered in Memphis on April 4, 1968. It happened just a few days before he was scheduled to speak to our denomination's General Assembly gathering in Minneapolis. I learned of the assassination from a ministerial colleague who called me, and I in turn broke the news to the bridge club members whom Robbie happened to be hosting in our home.

I kept my distance from all the confusion that marked the next days in Atlanta. However, soon after Dr. King's funeral, Ralph David Abernathy requested that the United Presbyterian Church make me available to the Southern

Christian Leadership Conference for three months to assist with fundraising from the Christian church community.

It was a well-intended but naïve notion. Only a few denominations responded with modest contributions to the written solicitations that we sent over Dr. Abernathy's signature. Our offer to follow up with face-to-face meetings yielded no replies. Other respondents politely replied that they would consider the request for assistance during their next budget cycle. Still others had their own ideas about how they preferred to honor Dr. King. Our appeals were further weakened because we failed to specify how the fund we requested would be used. Finally, it became clear that three months was far too short a period during which to identify, cultivate, and solicit prospective donors. We shelved the plan.

Ever since our arrival in Atlanta, Robbie and I had assumed that we would stay there for the foreseeable future. However, Gay Wilmore had other plans for me. The work of the Council on Church and Race was expanding, and he needed someone to come to New York and direct its operations. When the Southern Regional Council countered by offering me a position, I let myself be tempted briefly by this offer to remain in Atlanta. However, after further deliberation, Robbie and I began to prepare for a return to the New York area.

A few final thoughts about the Council on Church and Race are in order. Its formation is a reminder of the continual need for Christian communities to confront injustice. It came into being during the bursting forth of the American civil rights movement. The patterns of race relations were changing in both significant and superficial ways. Riots erupted in urban ghettos around the country. Prize-winning Black Olympic athletes raised their fists in defiant gestures. African-American women staged their own beauty pageants. Television viewers witnessed the broadcast of the first inter-racial kiss by Captain Kirk and Lieutenant Uhura. The activity and visibility of the Black Panther Party spread, and new Black-managed businesses and not-for-profit agencies came into being.

Drawing upon advocacy, education, and policy making, the Council on Church and Race played a major role in guiding my denomination toward a more inclusive and equitable future.

The work of the Council was not uniformly accepted. Portions of the church membership, especially those with long-established patterns of racial segregation, resisted the Council's calls for integration and justice and chose to leave the denomination. However, the Council's efforts clearly brought more people of color into positions of church leadership, promoted interracial communication, and prompted greater prophetic witness by the church in all matters of social justice.

And yet, despite the progress being made in the improvement of race relations, many people of color remained understandably impatient about the rate of change. One of the most dramatic examples of this resentment was the *Black Manifesto*—a demand for $500 million in reparations for 400 years of injustice suffered by African Americans. On Sunday, May 4, 1969, James Forman commandeered the pulpit of Riverside Church during the morning worship service to read the 2,500-word indictment of white churches and synagogues for their role in the persecution of Black people. The *Manifesto*, an official statement of the National Black Economic Development Conference, ignited a firestorm of debate that continues to this day.

Gay Wilmore, who composed a powerful endorsement of this Black declaration, arranged to have Forman speak to the General Assembly of the United Presbyterian Church USA (which had convened in San Antonio, Texas, a few days after his presentation at Riverside Church). An impressive demonstration occurred when all Black commissioners to the conference and Black staff members arranged to have themselves seated behind Forman in a sign of solidarity.

Like most of the major church groups, the United Presbyterian Church USA did not respond to the challenge of the Black Manifesto with a major contribution. However, a year later, the General Assembly authorized the creation of a new ministry called the Self-Development of People. Its goal was to assist economically poor, oppressed, and disadvantaged people to develop long-term, community-controlled projects like agricultural cooperatives and community organizing initiatives. Most of the funding came from the denomination's annual One Great Hour of Sharing offering.

9

New Occasions, New Duties

ONCE I AGREED TO JOIN the New York-based staff of the Council on Church and Race, my family and I began our search for a new residence. After considering a variety of options, we decided to settle in Teaneck, New Jersey. It was a well-established town that had grown steadily since the opening of the nearby George Washington Bridge in 1931. No one is certain whether its name originated in Native American or Dutch language, but it was known as a middle-class, predominantly white community whose population was about one-fourth Jewish. An unspoken demographic feature of the town was the maintenance of an all-Black middle-class section into which we moved.

Among Teaneck's appeals to us was its excellent public school system which had been one of the first in the country to desegregate voluntarily in 1965. It also included a special education division. We placed Cassandra in kindergarten, and she stayed enrolled in the same educational network until her graduation from high school in 1983 and her matriculation at Spelman College in Atlanta. Michelle, who remained developmentally delayed, spent most of the first 18 years of her life in special education programs in Teaneck and then nearby Fairlawn, New Jersey.

Our move from Atlanta went smoothly. The Rev. Bryant George, a good friend and colleague who lived in the area, helped us to find our first house. Other friends who were on vacation offered us the use of their home while we waited for our furniture to arrive.

I first met Bryant George while we were still living in Raleigh, but his reputation preceded him. A third-generation Presbyterian minister, he grew up on the Johnson C. Smith University campus where his father was a professor and dean of the seminary. Bryant completed his undergraduate studies there and then earned his divinity degree from McCormick Theological Seminary in Chicago. At the time we met, he was the highest ranking Black national staff member in the United Presbyterian Board of National Missions—someone with whom Black Presbyterian pastors were wise to cultivate relationships. Our early interaction was a bit chilly, perhaps because I was not one of the "Southern brothers" who had graduated from Johnson C. Smith College or Seminary and had advanced without the benefit of that connection. However, we grew steadily closer as I became increasingly involved in the denomination's national staff.

As a leader in the civil rights movement, he was a gifted strategist and church politician, who also had a love of classical music and an irrepressibly puckish sense of humor. We remained friends until his death in 2007.

Having a home close to New York meant that I had a relatively easy commute to my Manhattan office in the 475 Riverside Drive building. Since my work involved a lot of long-distance travel, it also helped me to live fairly close to Newark airport. Another bonus for all of us was the proximity of the Presbyterian Church of Teaneck, in whose programs we became active. We settled into our Cape Cod-style home, and I began planting a 20' x 20' garden with green beans, tomatoes, cucumbers, corn, and other vegetables.

When my family and I relocated to New Jersey, change had been a hallmark of the United Presbyterian Church, USA, for nearly a decade. It was driven by many factors, but the primary force was the shifting patterns of race relations in the United States and, indeed, the world.

At the denominational level, the creation of the Commission on Religion and Race in 1963 had signaled the church's increasing readiness to acknowledge its participation in the perpetuation of racism. Then in 1968, the Commission (whose staff I would soon join) became the Council on Church and Race.

A critically important survey by the new Council was a study of the General Assembly's three major agencies: the Commission on Ecumenical Mission and Relations (a successor to the Board of Foreign Mission), the Board of National Missions, and the Board of Christian Education. All three of them paid lip service to the work of the Council, but their support was not always evident. The Council retained a human relations consultant who was a Presbyterian elder from Detroit to study the staffing patterns of the three agencies. His report revealed that not one of the three agencies employed a single racial/ethnic person at the highest administrative level. One of them had only two Black staff members in supervisory positions. The only agency that had multiple racial/ethnic employees had just one staff person of color in its national office.

These findings generated a tidal wave of defensive reaction during a meeting of the Council members. Most of them resisted having the survey's findings reported to the forthcoming General Assembly. However, several agency heads immediately committed themselves to change their hiring practices and internal promotion policies. One of them was Donald Black.

Donald Black was General Secretary of the Commission on Ecumenical Mission and Relations—a long-time veteran of work at the local, national, and international levels. He immediately set out to recruit me as one of his two top associates.

Although very nervous, I survived an interview with the search committee in Chicago during the 1970 General Assembly in May and was invited to become a candidate for the position. However, since my selection would depend upon being elected by the entire Commission, Don decided that I would benefit from a "familiarization" experience to strengthen my knowledge of the field. He sent me on a whirlwind trip through Central America to meet mission personnel and partner churches.

My first visit was in Mexico City with Ben Gutierrez, the knowledgeable Latin American Secretary for both the United Presbyterian Church, USA, and the Presbyterian Church, USA, who held dual American and Mexican citizenship.

My orientation trip next took me to Guatemala where the United Presbyterian Church had a large number of workers who were responsible for churches, schools, and a unique seminary extension program. Their constituents were more indigenous and rural than the more urban populations in Mexico.

In San Jose, the capital of Costa Rica, the personnel I met focused their work on operating a Spanish language school for mission personnel from various denominations.

This hurried exposure to a portion of the mission field was sufficient to support my unanimous election to become COEMAR's Associate General Secretary for Africa and Latin America.

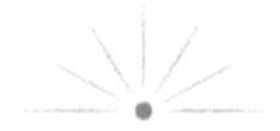

My next assignment began almost immediately: representatives of the Ethiopian Mission requested my help to reduce growing tension between the Ethiopian Christians and American mission workers. In short order I was flying over much of rural Ethiopia in a single-engine plane on visits to various outposts. As best I could determine from my meetings with local Christians, the tension among the missionaries stemmed primarily from the reluctance of the Americans to share leadership with the Ethiopians. Some of the Americans, especially those who had spent their entire professional careers in Ethiopia, feared that their careers would be terminated if they gave up their dominant positions.

After reading my report of the visit (which clearly sided with the feeling of the local Christians, Don discouraged me from sharing it with anyone, fearing that it would simply exaggerate tensions in a "no-win" situation.

In any event, my position as Associate General Secretary was short-lived. Within a few months, the Commission ceased to exist, and its work was assumed by the new Program Agency.

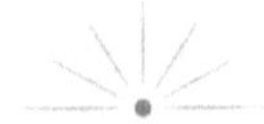

The Program Agency, created by the 1972 General Assembly, was designed to be one of three new core units of the denomination's administration. Prior to our organizational revision, we had been a web of separate boards and agencies, each separate for a specific domain (e.g., world missions, national missions, Christian education, stewardship). In the new version, all programmatic activity was clustered into one structure called the Program Agency. Functions having to do with leadership, personnel, and training were clustered into another organization called the Vocation Agency. Finally, all work that supported the Program and Vocation Agencies (e.g., income, purchasing, disbursements, accounting, travel, shipping) were clustered in the Support Agency.

It is difficult to capture all the elements and many details of the reconstituted denomination, but it was a more streamlined structure. It also emphasized mission and social justice and sought to focus resources and leadership on priority areas like racial equality, urban ministry, global partnerships, and ecumenical outreach. The new Program Agency was intended to give special attention to the voices of marginalized communities, within both the Church and the broader society. Furthermore, it encouraged regular communication, open hearings, and more opportunities for grassroots input to national decision-making. All these changes constituted a major shake-up, but they held the promise of yielding increased efficiency, quicker responses to emerging or changing needs, and a renewed sense of unity and purpose throughout the denomination.

There were three finalists (two African Americans and one white man) to become the General Director of the new Program Agency: my good friend Bryant George, Don Black, (my "boss"), and I. In his usual whimsical fashion, Bryant was quick to point out that "one way or the other, they're going to elect someone Black."

Both Don and Bryant had far more administrative and management experience than I, and both were better known throughout the denomination. On the other hand, I was the only candidate who had been a staff member for each of the former agencies (National Missions, Christian Education, and Ecumenical Mission and Relations) without being closely identified with any of them. At thirty-six years old, I also was the youngest of the candidates.

What could have been an even more serious barrier to my selection was my involvement in a controversial decision—a grant from the Council on Church and Race to the legal defense fund for Angela Davis. Professor Davis, a former faculty member at UCLA was an avowed member of the American Communist Party and had close ties to members of the Black Panther Party. She had been arrested when guns registered to her were used in the murder of a U.S. judge. The case became a national *cause celebre* after St. Andrew Presbyterian Church in Marin City, California, petitioned the Synod of the of the Golden Gate, (whose associate executive was my friend, Gene Turner) to help fund her legal defense. At my direction, the Council on Church and Race approved the grant of $10,000, which was channeled through that synod to Davis's legal team. More than 6,000 letters of protest poured into the national offices of the denomination.

The 1972 General Assembly questioned the propriety of the decision but chose not to reverse it. After the furor about

the grant subsided, a group of us Black Presbyterian ministers personally contributed a total of $10,000 to repay the
funds that had been allotted. Our action was not intended
to refund the grant to the Angela Davis Defense Fund but
rather to affirm our faith in the Black community.

At any rate, Angela Davis was acquitted, and my can-
didacy for the Program Agency position remained intact.
Later reflecting aloud upon the experience during an interview, I described it as an occasion when I witnessed United
Presbyterians at both their best and their worst.

Someone has written "Friendship is the mystery of chance
encounters, shared laughter, and the weaving of countless
small moments into something enduring." That definition
accurately describes my friendship with Gene Turner.

When I first met the soft-spoken Gene during the early
1960s as fellow members of Black Presbyterians United, he
was on the staff of the Presbytery of Philadelphia, and I was
working for the Council on Church and Race. We were both
native Georgians but seemingly had little in common.

Gene was from Macon where he graduated from the
Ballard-Hudson School, the only high school for Black
students in that city. His father had his own logging business
and his family lived in its own home. As I have already

described, the first property my sharecropper father ever owned was a used bicycle, and the McClouds lived in an unpainted shack without electricity on a plantation that was miles from the nearest town.

Gene completed undergraduate studies at Knoxville College, a historically Black institution and served in the U.S. Army before doing further theological study at Pittsburgh Theological Seminary and taking courses in ethics and government at Harvard University. After serving pastorates in Patterson, New Jersey, and Pittsburgh, he joined the Philadelphia Presbytery staff.

Gene subsequently went to work for the Synod of the Golden Gate on the West Coast (our relationship deepened during the Angela Davis controversy that I have already described) and later became the Executive of the Northeast Synod in upstate New York.

My international involvement in ecumenical affairs gave me the opportunity of introducing Gene to the World Council of Churches when he joined me on a trip to Jamaica for a meeting of the WCC's Central Committee (of which he too later became a member). He and I spent a great deal of time together during the 1970s and 1980s, not just on fishing expeditions but also in deep conversations about current affairs and theology.

Eventually Gene became the Associate Stated Clerk of the denomination's General Assembly, and, as ecumenical officer, represented the denomination at the National Council of

Churches, the World Council of Churches, and the World Alliance of Reformed Churches.

On a balmy September afternoon, I was with my daughters in the backyard of our Teaneck home when Robbie called me to the telephone. The Program Agency search committee had selected me as its nominee. I was to assume my new position on November 1, 1972. Thus began the most exciting, mind-stretching, challenging and life-changing 14 years of my life.

(After he was not selected to lead the Program Agency, Don Black accepted the call to become pastor of The American Church in London. He remained in that position until I hired my former "boss" to be my associate in 1977. Then, after our denomination merged with the Presbyterian Church in the U.S. in 1983, Don was elected as the first executive director of its General Assembly Council. He retired in 1988. Bryant George went on to take a position in New York with The Ford Foundation and subsequently headed U.S. Agency for International Development (USAID) operations in the Philippines.)

A fundamental commitment in the reorganization of the denomination's administration was the encouragement of non-white executive leadership—a concept to which I was deeply committed. However, by the second year of my tenure, my good intentions were put to the test as we confronted the need for some major budget reductions. I made it clear to everyone in the Program Agency that the process called for all divisions to reduce their staffs and budgets. One of the few Black directors at that time dug in his heels and adamantly refused to follow that direction. When further discussion, persuasion, and negotiation failed, and he refused to follow orders, I fired him. Word of my action spread rapidly; a group of Black Presbyterian leaders summoned me to a private meeting and sought an explanation for my decision, especially in light of the small number of executives of color on the Program Agency staff. Once I made it clear that I had terminated the employee for insubordination, the matter was dropped. However, my reputation for tough, color-blind management was established.

As noted, the Program Agency was a complex cluster of programs whose collective budget exceeded $30 million and included the Westminster Press publishing unit. One of my first challenges was to staff the new system with a combination of both existing and new employees of the Church. The process of assembling a new leadership team—especially during the discovery in the second year that we faced a budget crisis, was an experience that I would prefer never to repeat, but in the process we created a strong new administrative structure.

It became clear that I needed a senior administrator on my staff who would be responsible for day-to-day operations while I maintained relations with presbyteries, synods, overseas partner churches, the National Council of Churches, and the World Council of Churches—a responsibility that kept me away from the office at least one-third of the time.

While our denomination was reconstructing its organizational framework, a special committee that included Gayraud Wilmore had been tackling a more theological challenge: the composition of what was to become the Confession of 1967. The turbulent decade of the 1960s had challenged church bodies everywhere to restate their faith, and this seven-year process produced the first statement of its kind since the Westminster Confession of Faith was adopted three centuries earlier. After lengthy discussion and revisions, more than 90 percent of the presbyteries voted approval, and final adoption came at the 179th General Assembly of the United Presbyterian Church, USA in 1967.

Even as we still were getting the Program Agency organized, I was called in 1973 to join an official, bi-racial denominational delegation to South Africa. The Dutch Reformed Church of that country wanted to discuss and presumably learn from our experience with the composition of the new confessional document. Our group included Clinton Marsh, the recently elected Moderator of the General Assembly, his wife Agnes, theological professors, church officials and several of my board members. We were divided into smaller groups, and I was assigned the leadership of the group dispatched to the East Coast City of Durban.

It was an eye-opening experience to visit this country that had established and refined the system of racial separation known as *apartheid*. I learned that the only way I was permitted to be registered in our hotel was to have myself classified as an "Honorary White" individual—a bizarre designation that I did not find to be a flattering description.

While in Durban I spotted a bulletin board announcement that Chief Mongosuthulu Buthelezi was scheduled to speak to a conference group in our hotel. From my reading about South Africa, I knew this Zulu prince to be one of the most prominent politicians and leaders in the country. I sent him a note expressing my desire to meet him and was delighted when he invited me to join him for coffee.

It was virtually impossible to visit South Africa without recalling the Sharpeville Massacre of 1960—a defining moment in the country's history when police killed 69 Black protestors of apartheid and injured 180 others. Later that year the World Council of Churches had convened a conference in the Johannesburg suburb of Cottesloe to protest the massacre.

Our well-intended visit to South Africa was inconclusive. I returned to the United States keenly aware that white South Africans lived in fear of their country's Black majority and Black South Africans could only hope for a better day.

My connection with South Africa deepened as I became acquainted with Desmond Tutu. When I first met him at a World Council of Churches gathering in Geneva, Switzerland, he was an Anglican priest who already was making a name for himself by his outspoken opposition to apartheid. Our paths continued to cross at gatherings of liberation groups like the African National Congress in Zambia, Zimbabwe, and South Africa. The purpose of these meetings was for American and European church representatives to learn about the groups'

strategies to gain freedom and to reaffirm support for their struggle. The liberation groups always urged us to put pressure on our respective governments to discontinue economic support for repressive regimes. Trans-Africa (which I will later describe) was one of the American responses in support of liberation efforts. Another example was the World Council of Churches Program to Combat Racism which provides financial support for the liberation groups.

Within a few years Tutu had become the General Secretary of the South African Council of Churches and an even more annoying thorn in the side of the racist South African government. In response, the authorities established a judicial inquiry to investigate the SACC's finances. The Eloff Commission, which took its name from the presiding judge, sought to establish that the South African organization had misused the funds donated to it. As evidence of its "fairness," it sought testimony from financial supporters in the United States and Europe. The National Council of Churches responded by sending as its representatives a white pastor with Dutch ancestry (the Rev. Arie Brouwer from the Reformed Church of American) and me (a descendant of enslaved Africans). We rejected the commission's assertion of financial wrongdoing, and its inability to document misconduct proved to be of great embarrassment to the South African government. Among the points we stressed was the argument that the South African organization was responsible not to American funders but to Almighty God.

It was an admittedly rare occasion but there was an incident when the international outreach of the Program Agency resembled a scene from a *Mission Impossible* television episode. A Presbyterian missionary had been kidnapped by Ethiopian rebels and held several weeks for ransom. Advised by the U.S. government not to pay the $150,000 demanded for his release, the Program Agency offered instead to deliver a planeload of food to the kidnappers. However, aboard the aircraft that was sent were both Ethiopian and U.S. military personnel. Upon arrival, they engaged in gunfire that killed several of the rebels and rescued the missionary.

In 1975 I had the privilege of serving as one of the United Presbyterian Church delegates to the Fifth Assembly of the World Council of Churches in the beautiful city of Nairobi, Kenya. During the course of the conference, I first met representatives from the Reformed Presbyterian Church of Cuba. The Cuban revolution had severed what had been a 50-year relationship between the Presbyterians of both countries, one in which the Cuban church was a presbytery of the Synod of New Jersey. Seeing an opportunity to rebuild some of the lost connections, I hosted a dinner for the two delegations and set in motion a rebuilding of relationships that continues to the present.

Among the most positive outcomes of the renewed connection was the restoration of pension funds owed to retired Cuban Presbyterian church workers that had been "frozen" after the Cuban revolution.

My presence at the Nairobi convocation set in motion a series of life-changing experiences for me. I was elected to the Central Committee and the Executive Committee of the World Council and six years later became Moderator of the Central Committee's Finance Committee—a series of responsibilities that continued even after my work with the Program Agency ended. Having the privilege and responsibility of observing the denomination's work elsewhere in the world was an invaluable gift.

Among my myth-shattering experiences was the opportunity to visit with Christians living under authoritarian regimes. Spending time with Christians in East Germany, Poland,

Hungary, and Czechoslovakia gave me a new appreciation of the casual way in which we Americans assume the availability of religious freedom. (One of the highlights of that trip was the privilege of spending time with the widow of Josef Hromadka, the renowned Lutheran pastor and Czech Protestant theologian.)

My efforts to visit China with a group from Harvard University failed when my visa was denied. However, a second chance arose when the Christian Council of China (yes, such an organization exists) invited a visit from the U.S. National Council of Churches, and I was invited to be a member of the delegation. Since the United States did not have diplomatic relations with the People's Republic of China at that time, we flew to Hong Kong and traveled by train from there into China.

U.S. passports in those days had printed in them the names of countries for which the passport was not valid for travel. China was on that list. However, at the crossing into China from Hong Kong, immigration officials simply stapled our visas into our passports. When we departed, they unfastened the staples documents, leaving no evidence that we had used our passports for travel to China.

Our impressions from the trip (which included a visit to the Great Wall) were of extremely friendly Chinese

Christians, vibrant church gatherings that attracted families with many children, and the vast number of people and bicycles on the streets of Shanghai and Beijing.

One of the most nerve-wracking periods of my time as head of the Program Agency began in May 1984, when the Rev. Ben Weir, a long-time Presbyterian missionary in Beirut, Lebanon, was kidnapped by Hezbollah radicals and placed in squalid solitary confinement for 16 months. His captivity made national headlines, and the persistence of his wife, Carol, triggered the sending of so many thousands of messages from members of the United Presbyterian Church and other Americans to President Ronald Reagan that the White House had to secure the services of additional secretarial help. Our Program Agency staff engaged in intense negotiations with the U.S. Department of State until Weir's release was secured. (The entire complex process, which came to be known as the Iran/Contra affair, was interwoven with the U.S. sale of arms to the rebels and the use of those proceeds to fund opposition to the socialist revolutionaries who were controlling the government of Nicaragua.)

Soon after Weir's release, he was elected Moderator of the 1986 General Assembly.

Much of my schedule was consumed by a seemingly unending round of both domestic and international travel. However, two of the highlights of our years in New Jersey were family vacation trips. The one in 1971 was to the Walt Disney World Resort in Florida, where Cassandra developed an insatiable appetite for riding the Space Mountain roller coaster, and I'm determined never to climb on it again. Another was a five-week, cross-country trek in a Winnebago that we borrowed from a minister-friend. That van transported us through the Black Hills of South Dakota and the Grand Tetons and took us to the Old Faithful geyser in Yellowstone National Park before delivering us to Disneyland and San Francisco and carrying us into the Mojave Desert. The most highly adver-tised (mile after mile of roadside signage) and most disap-pointing stop on the trip was the visit to the Corn Palace in Mitchell, South Dakota.

During these years, our relationship with the Costens con-tinued to be close. I cannot describe it without adding some reference to the remarkable Melva. The child of a Presbyterian family of long standing in Due West, South Carolina, she first completed her studies at Harbison Junior College before continuing her education at Johnson C. Smith University. It was there that she met and married Jim in the university chapel. Despite functioning as a pastor's wife and the mother of his children, she continued to develop her already considerable musical talents, later earning degrees at the University of North Carolina and Georgia State University.

Because she was a gifted choral conductor and arranger, her name quickly came to mind when the Program Agency and the General Assembly Mission Board set about the task of creating a new hymnal for the denomination. I happily accepted the enjoyable task of recruiting her to lead that challenging project by telephoning the Costen household. Jim answered the phone. After learning the purpose of my call, he assured me that his wife was too busy to accept the offer. Nonetheless, he said, she could speak for herself.

When I told Melva the purpose of my call, she accepted the opportunity with enormous enthusiasm. She then went on to chair a richly diverse 18-person committee that created *The Presbyterian Hymnal: Hymns, Psalms and Spiritual Songs (1990)*. I will add only that the solemn reverence in which she held her musical and racial heritage was balanced by a boisterous sense of humor.

When she died in 2023, it became my sad responsibility to preside over the celebration of her life—a memorial service marked by a lengthy procession of people who wanted to step forward and voice their tributes to her.

Soon after Jimmy Carter's election to the U.S. presidency in 1976, I traveled to India where our denomination had maintained a long and positive presence in the fields of both health and education. One of its most renowned institutions was the health center in Pune—deservedly celebrated for its pioneering work in preventive medicine.

A highlight of that time in India was the visit with Prime Minister Indira Gandhi that our denominational representative arranged for me. I distinctly recall her pleasure when she exclaimed, "How wonderful that the United States has elected a peanut farmer as President."

The visit to India also included an overnight train trip from New Delhi to a college in Amritsar, established by the Presbyterian Church. I and three colleagues had reserved a sleeper cabin with four bunks and were taken aback when a total stranger was assigned to the empty space. Even as I was dealing with that surprise, our travel representative informed me that I was expected to deliver an address to a college convocation the next day. Equipped with only a yellow pad and pen, I was somehow inspired by the Spirit to compose a message that won applause...although I still have no memory of what I said.

The cover of the January 1982 edition of *United Presbyterian A.D.*, a glossy magazine printed by my denomination, featured a close-up picture of me, further amplified by a lengthy interview on the inside of the publication. In a sense, it was a 10-year review of my work as head of the Program Agency. Curiously, the only two photographs of me presented me standing on the deck of a U.S. Navy aircraft carrier and receiving an award from Berea College, my undergraduate alma mater.

Had the editors chosen to take notice of all the countries I visited during my days with the Program Agency, they might well have used the entire magazine. In addition to the many nations and kingdoms already mentioned, my travels carried me to all the Scandinavian countries, Portugal, the Netherlands, Iceland, and Zaire. Also on my itinerary were Argentina, Brazil, Colombia; Egypt and Lebanon; Pakistan, Taiwan, and Thailand.

The World Council of Churches assembly in Vancouver in 1983 was the first to be held in Canada and only the second in North America. It provided me with the opportunity to assist people with special needs like my older daughter. Working with United Presbyterian Women and the Stony Point Center, I arranged for the Program Agency to purchase a van that was equipped to transport handicapped conference attendees. I recruited two seminary students to drive the vehicle to Vancouver and operate it during the 10-day conference, after which it became the property of the retreat center. (In subsequent years, the two students from Johnson C. Smith Theological Seminary became Presbyterian pastors and one of them was chosen to be a Presbytery executive.)

Willis Logan from the National Council of Churches and I were among the small group of Americans invited by Desmond Tutu to attend his enthronement as Bishop of Johannesburg in 1985. The service began with Tutu, (who had been awarded the Nobel Peace Prize the year before) following an *a cappella* choir of ululating and dancing Black Africans down the center aisle and then delivering a powerful, hour-long sermon. A year later, he was elected Archbishop of Cape Town, the highest Anglican position in South Africa.

Several years later I had the privilege of being the only American in a small World Council of Churches delegation to the 1990 Rustenburg Conference of Black and white church leaders from many denominations in South Africa. The historic gathering in a town 80 miles northwest of Johannesburg produced a historic document that denounced *apartheid* as a sin.

One of the most powerful moments of the conference occurred when an Afrikaner (i.e., a white South African delegate) publicly confessed his guilt for having supported *apartheid* and asked his Black fellow Christians for forgiveness. His confession prompted a furious young Black Anglican priest to reject the confession. This reaction brought Archbishop Tutu to his feet; in a soft, pastoral tone he publicly admonished his young colleague and questioned how a Christian could refuse to accept the admission of sin by a fellow Christian.

The conference concluded with the adoption of a declaration approved by the delegates that expressed contrition for the sins of the past and a call for action to repair those wrongs.

At the conclusion of the gathering, our delegation had the opportunity of a brief visit with Nelson and Winnie Mandela. He had only recently been released from 27 years of imprisonment. The calmness and humility that this tall, soft-spoken modern-day hero projected made an indelible impression on me and moved me to tears. I concluded that had he been a Roman Catholic, he would have been elevated to sainthood.

10

Preparing Our Successors

B Y 1986 I HAD BEEN with the Program Agency since November 1972 and was serving my third five-year term. Few people, including several of my board members, would have predicted that I could survive the turbulence that had marked the restructuring of the entire denomination when I began my tour of duty. However, I had successfully managed the largest agency in the history of our denomination with a staff of more than 250 employees. In the process I had earned the respect of many of the church's fraternal workers (as they were called at the time) as well as our overseas partner churches.

Furthermore, my denomination and the Presbyterian Church, U.S, had succeeded in achieving reunion and the thought of being involved in the turbulence of another major re-organization held no appeal. I had informed my board members that I had no intention of completing my term. Nonetheless, I was open to new possibilities.

One interesting inquiry had come from the pastor and an Elder at Fourth Presbyterian Church in Chicago. That large congregation was prepared to pay a generous salary to someone who could direct a program of outreach to the Cabrini-Green neighborhood, the massive and deeply troubled public housing project on the near north side of the city. The dynamics of a rich white church in the heart of Chicago's Magnificent Mile suddenly becoming the partner of a poor, all-Black district may have been well-intended, but to me it seemed destined to fail. At the very least, any success was likely to consume a great deal of energy and other resources.

Robbie came up with a quick way to resolve the question about whether I should pursue the Chicago overture: after researching winter weather conditions in Chicago, she emphatically blocked any further consideration of the idea.

I also was asked to apply for the presidency of two seminaries. However, it seemed fairly clear to me that they needed a Black candidate primarily to document that their search had been racially inclusive.

Knowing that I was serious about finding a new position, Robbie made clear her preference for us to remain in New Jersey. It was at that point that I heard from Robert Williams, a professor at Washington University in St. Louis, who was chair of the search committee of The Fund for Theological Education (FTE).

FTE had come into existence in 1954—a time when a variety of factors had left large numbers of Protestant pulpits unfilled. Financially underwritten by the wealth of the Rockefeller family, the new program had played a key role in increasing the number and quality of college graduates pursuing theological education and entering the parish ministry. Its early trustees included Nathan Pusey, President of Harvard University, and Benjamin Mays, the well-known and esteemed President of Morehouse College.

I was a bit baffled when first approached about my interest in becoming the Executive Director of the Fund. I should have suspected that Jim Costen had something to do with the inquiry. Sure enough, I soon discovered that my close friend was a member of the search committee that was seeking a new administrator of the organization.

I wasn't hostile to the notion. Several of my classmates at Union had been so-called "Rockefeller Fellows" (receiving tuition and living expenses to underwrite an exploratory first year at seminary), and I knew that the Fund was based in Princeton. Otherwise, my knowledge of it was severely limited. Nonetheless, I agreed to meet with the committee. Our conversation was pleasant and informative, but I left the meeting with no sense that anything substantive had been accomplished.

It shocked me when the search committee subsequently asked me to outline the conditions under which I would consider accepting the FTE leadership position. The proposed salary was significantly less than what I was earning, but I had to take seriously the fact that the job could keep my family in northern New Jersey. On the other hand, I wasn't thrilled by the prospect of a daily 100-mile, round-trip commute by car to and from Princeton. Finally, although that town's university ambience was charming, I would derive little benefit from my surroundings: the FTE office was in a nondescript office complex on the outskirts of the historic town.

What finally triggered my decision was the committee's assurance that I could move the office to any location that offered easy access to an airport. I accepted the job offer and began work in July 1986, all the while pondering a change in office location.

It didn't take long to determine that the ideal office space would be at the Interchurch Center, not simply because of its proximity to my home but because I felt that we needed to be in close touch with the many denominations whose ministerial candidates we were supporting. That decision did not sit well with the Associate Director who resigned and demanded a generous severance payment to compensate her for her many years in that position. I let the board negotiate the terms of her departure, and we relocated the office to New York City. My daily commute was no longer a burdensome trek.

A greater challenge involved the building of increased financial support for the basic fellowship program as well as for new ventures—particularly a Black doctoral fellowship program, and programs in urban ministry and Hispanic ministry. The organization whose leadership I inherited had an Associate Director position (now vacated) and a secretary, a budget of less than $500,000, and no prospects of any long-range financial support. My principal occupation was now to function as the organization's chief fundraiser. In the pursuit of new support, I was helped enormously by Robert Lynn, the Lilly Endowment vice president who had been my dean at Auburn Seminary and by the Pew Charitable Trusts.

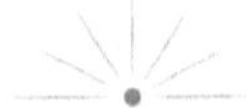

It was a busy period for our family. Even as I was settling into my new position, Cassandra was entering her senior year at Spelman College in Atlanta. Watched by proud family members, our younger daughter received her diploma during a commencement ceremony at which Lena Horne was the principal speaker in the spring of 1987. That fall Cassandra began her studies at the law school of the University of Maryland in Baltimore.

One of my first moves at the Fund was to convene a consultation on urban ministry that included seminary educators, urban ministers, community leaders, and denominational representatives. A major outcome of that gathering was a new, two-part program. The first component provided fellowships for seminarians to pursue internships in urban settings that the Fund established. The second part was an FTE-funded continuing education program for clergy and ministerial teams. The $2.3 million from the Lilly Endowment that underwrote the cost of this new program was the largest single grant ever received by the Fund.

We also built upon an earlier study of Hispanic theological education by Justo Gonzalez, a Cuban-American historical theologian and Methodist Elder in Atlanta. His work helped us to secure funding from the Pew Charitable Trusts to underwrite significantly increased support for Hispanic ministerial and doctoral programs, and we hired Benjamin Alicea, a former FTE Fellow to manage those initiatives.

Other foundation grants as well as support from individuals, congregations, and denominations supported our development efforts and increased our funding of women's theological scholarships. We felt further empowered to convene a consultation on Asian ministry.

With the aid of the Lilly Endowment and other supporters, the organization re-invented itself and found stability.

I felt that I had served the purpose for which I had been hired. It seemed to be a good time to pursue other challenges.

After my departure, the organization went through a difficult organizational and financial period. However, now known as the Forum for Theological Exploration and based in Decatur, Georgia, it continues to be a major resource for the preparation of Christian leaders in the parish, academia, and the broader community.

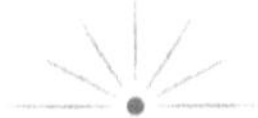

During my time at the Fund, Willis Logan, Director of the Africa office for the National Council of Churches, recruited me to the board of TransAfrica. It was an advocacy group that sought to influence U.S. foreign policy toward African and Caribbean countries. Founded in 1977 by Randall Robinson, an African American graduate of Virginia Union University and Harvard Law School, it was the largest and oldest social justice organization in the United States that focused on the African world.

One strategy with which we sought to call attention to South Africa's *apartheid* system was to dispatch board members and other supporters to picket that country's embassy in Washington on a regular basis. In due course, on a day of protesting in 1990, we failed to disperse as ordered by the police. We were arrested, handcuffed, loaded into a paddy wagon, taken to a local precinct, charged with trespassing, and released on $50 bail. When we appeared in court as ordered the next morning, the judge dismissed the charges against us.

After all my years of civil rights activity, it was the first and only time I was apprehended by the police. I still treasure the experience, plastic handcuffs and all. I also find it ironic that my arrest was for opposition to racism in a foreign country and not segregation in the United States.

11

Never Say 'Never'

THREE DECADES HAD ELAPSED SINCE I left the parish ministry. I had long ago stopped speculating about a return to a local church. I was even more certain that I never wanted to be part of a multi-staff pastorate for a large congregation. Nonetheless, on January 21, 1996, I was installed as the Associate Pastor of Administration at Fifth Avenue Presbyterian Church in New York City. My long-time mentor, Gayraud Willmore, preached the sermon on that occasion. Once again, I discovered the folly of saying "never."

This unexpected turn of events started when Tom Tewell, the relatively new pastor at Fifth Avenue Presbyterian Church in New York, sought the advice of James Costen, then the president of the Interdenominational Theological Center in Atlanta. Tewell had come to his position from the leadership of Memorial Drive Presbyterian Church in Houston, Texas. There he had been instrumental in increasing the size of the membership to more than five thousand people, and he already was attracting new members to the historic New York church.

Tewell explained to Costen that he was looking for an associate pastor to oversee the administration of his congregation and supervise the non-pastoral portion of his 30-member staff. Costen immediately responded that a suitable candidate with executive experience—one Oscar McCloud—was Tewell's neighbor right there in New York. Tewell wasted no time in reaching out to me.

My subsequent lunch with him and a meeting with the search committee went well; apparently my theological defense of baptism by complete bodily immersion intrigued several of the lay people. At any rate, I soon received a formal offer to join the staff.

The timing of Tewell's effort to recruit me could not have been better. Although I had enjoyed my work at the Fund for Theological Education, I also was aware that change might be in the offing. My board was contemplating the relocation of my office close to the headquarters of the Association of Theological Schools in Pittsburgh. I had no interest in leaving the New York metropolitan area.

I knew very little about the Fifth Avenue church. At that point I doubted that I had been inside the facility more than once or twice, if even that many times. To be sure, I was aware of its reputation. Many years earlier *TIME Magazine* had described it as the cathedral of Presbyterianism. It was the largest Presbyterian church in New York City and recognized for the excellence of its pastors' preaching as well as its musical programming. On December 26, 1965, Duke Ellington and his orchestra recorded their award-winning concert of sacred music in the large sanctuary. (In subsequent years, Dave Brubeck brought similar programs to the church, including a Christmas concert, *La Fiesta de la Poseda*, in 1985.)

Fifth Avenue Presbyterian, as befits an institution with its lengthy history, embraced a colorful collection of both solemn and quirky traditions and sets of behavior:

- ► In deference to the patients in a hospital that once stood across the street, the church's clock tower—the tallest structure in Manhattan at the time of its construction—never held a set of bells. However, its clockwork continued to be wound by hand every week.

- ► The congregation was still using a hymnal that had been published in 1933 and, consequently, included none of the texts and melodies of the past half-century.

- ► Access to the antique but effective heating and cooling system depended upon the use of a unique louvered system beneath the pews that an individual worshipper could activate with a touch of the foot.

▶ The church could lay claim to having been instrumental in the founding of Princeton Theological Seminary, the American Bible Society, New York Presbyterian Hospital, and numerous mission boards.

▶ And it had been in existence long enough to have weathered the pastoral terms of ministers who were both spiritual inspirations and sources of congregational division.

The church also had an extensive ministry to the city's homeless people. That commitment had triggered what became an ongoing legal battle with the City of New York over the right to permit destitute people to seek shelter in the church's entrances—a battle that the church won.

Tom Tewell had a passion for Christian education and organized the curriculum for everyone from children to senior citizens. He also had become a powerful and well-publicized proponent of greater inclusivity in the Church.

Based on what I already knew and quickly learned, it didn't take long before I accepted the offer to become a member of the church's professional leadership.

I had, of course, anticipated that the job description would include such traditional duties as budget development and staff oversight, as well as the responsibility to preach a few times each year and to assist with the leadership of worship. What I had not expected was that my new job would also involve a virtual crash course in civil engineering, architecture, construction, and city planning.

These subjects became important because the church had determined that it needed to expand its facilities. Taking a page from the experience of nearby Carnegie Hall with whose leadership we consulted, we decided to convert our church's undercroft (an Anglican word for basement) into a comprehensive Christian education center. The conversion of that space involved the excavation and removal of the 10 feet of solid granite on which the building rested as well as the renovation and air conditioning of the sanctuary and other portions of the church property—a massive and complicated undertaking.

The price tag for this enormous construction and restoration project was in excess of $30 million. Clearly, a major gifts campaign was going to be needed to reach that goal.

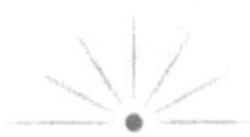

As a boy I had often gone fishing with my father and brothers in the many streams near our home in rural Georgia. Once I overcame the fear of drowning that I described earlier, I enjoyed filling our burlap bags with bass, catfish, crappies, and other freshwater fish.

After I left home, though, years passed before fishing re-entered my life. It took our move to New Jersey for my enjoyment of that pastime to resurface. The shift began on our trips from Teaneck to the Atlantic beaches (which the natives refer to as "The Shore"). There I discovered the joy of catching bluefish, a tasty migrating species with sharp teeth that grow quite large. I still have a picture of the first one I ever caught—a 15-pounder.

Then, when my family asked about my wishes for my 65th birthday, I blurted out a desire to go fishing for salmon in Alaska. Robbie and my daughters must have been startled by the request, but they dutifully lined up reservations for me at the Great Alaska Adventure Lodge.

That first escapade matured into a virtual obsession. For the next 15 years, often accompanied by my close friend, Gene Turner, or other colleagues and neighbors, I made an annual pilgrimage to the "last frontier." It was a vacation that included fishing for halibut some 10-15 miles off the Alaska coast or for salmon in the Kenai River. (I also have a picture of the largest I ever caught—a 54-pound king salmon.) Adding to my pleasure was the enjoyment of shipping home a portion of my catch to share with friends and neighbors.

Soon after I got "hooked" on deep sea fishing, I convinced Gene Turner (for whom angling of any kind was a foreign pastime) to join me first on my forays off the New Jersey coast and then on my regular visits to Alaska. His skills steadily graduated from those of an awkward novice to those of an accomplished fisherman. In the process of these regular excursions (including one to Costa Rica), we developed a great enjoyment of each other's company. We became best friends, more like brothers, visiting each other's homes, and being with each other in times of joy and sadness.

The closing of the lodge at which we stayed, and my advancing age, brought the scheduling of this annual excursion to an end, but happy memories of those great adventures still linger strongly.

As it did for most Americans, Tuesday, September 11, 2001, began as a routine day for me. I took Michelle to her day program at the Opportunity Center and then continued on my usual route toward Manhattan. The news on the radio began describing some kind of explosion at the World Trade Center, followed by the report of a plane flying into the South Tower. Then I encountered a flashing road signal that announced the closing of the George Washington Bridge. I managed to exit from a long line of traffic and return home. There I spent the rest of the day watching television news reports, crying, and calling my colleagues to check on their well-being.

I was able to get to the office the next day. The first order of business was to respond to the request that we send clergy to the Pierre Hotel. Pastors were needed to comfort the grieving family members of the Cantor Fitzgerald investment company employees who had been lost in the attack. It was a scene like nothing I had ever seen before or wish to see again; old and young people milling about, holding up pictures of their loved ones and asking about their whereabouts. My ministerial colleague, Jane Ammon, and I remained for an hour or so before realizing how little we could do and returned to the church.

However, we soon received a request to which we were able to respond: 67 of the 170 employees of Keefe, Bruyette & Woods, an investment bank in the World Trade Center, were lost in the attack. One of them was the co-founder, with his brother, of the company. The surviving brother requested through one of our church's elders whether Fifth Avenue would be willing to conduct a memorial service for the families of the victims. Since the surviving brother was a graduate of the illustrious Cardinal Spellman High School in the Bronx, he further inquired whether we would permit the Roman Catholic monsignor, principal of the school, to participate in the service.

Tom Tewell was out of town, so I made the decision to approve the requests. Furthermore, I scheduled the memorial ceremony for a Sunday afternoon in the main sanctuary and shifted our regular service at that time to the chapel. Since the Keefe Bruyette firm had many Irish Catholic employees, the memorial service was well attended.

A colleague of mine who had been scheduled to conduct the Sunday afternoon service complained about my decision to rearrange the church worship calendar, and Tom chided me publicly at the next staff meeting. However, on the first anniversary of the September 11 tragedy, we were asked to conduct another memorial service for the families of the company's employees. That service was also held in the main sanctuary, officiated by Tom Tewell, and participated in by the Cardinal Spellman High School principal, a Jewish rabbi, and me.

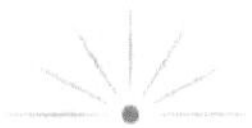

Robbie entered Hackensack Hospital on November 17, 2002, and died in her sleep 12 days later—the day after Thanksgiving. I spent most of her last nights with her. She was 65 years old. Her emphysema (diagnosed a decade earlier when she was hospitalized for bronchitis) had grown progressively worse. Robbie was a chronic cigarette smoker who simply could not break the habit. She also avoided visits with doctors—perhaps because she feared their evaluations of her condition. Both of her parents and two siblings had died while still relatively young.

Cassandra stayed with her mother during her last night, but Robbie never again saw the older daughter for whom she had cared since birth. When told that her mother had died, Michelle responded simply, "She will not be coming home."

The first of two memorial services for Robbie on Saturday, December 7, was well attended by family members and friends. It was held at the Presbyterian Church of Teaneck, where Robbie had been a member and our family worshiped. Gloria Tate, our pastor, presided, and Jim Costen, delivered the eulogy. Also taking part in the service were Cassandra and friends of Robbie. The entire ceremony, including the musical selections and musicians, reflected Robbie's careful choices. Her philosophy about services of remembrance had been summed up in one of her statements to me: "I don't need a service when I die, but you do."

Tom Tewell preached the eulogy during a similar service the next day at the Fifth Avenue church. Attending were many members of the congregation and other friends from New York City.

Robbie and I had decided a decade earlier that we would eventually need to place Michelle in a home for disabled people but could find nothing we deemed suitable in New Jersey or Georgia. However, with the help of John Evans, a Presbyterian Church US executive, we learned about Duvall Home in Glenwood, Florida. Our initial plan had called for me to retire and relocate with Robbie to Atlanta, at which time we would place Michelle at Duvall. Robbie's death delayed my retirement, and the next summer I took Michelle to Duvall. She lived there until we transferred her to a group home in New Jersey.

Offsetting the many gifts that came my way were the deep disappointments that I have described. One other sorrow requires mention. More than half a century ago, Robbie and I decided to share the blessings we had received by adopting a small boy. Tony Delancy was three years old when he came to live with us. He had spent the previous two and a half years with a loving white foster family that had three natural children. He adjusted well to his new environment, but his behavior began to change as he became a teenager. When he was 15 years old, he ran away from home and was arrested in New York City after attempting to break into a car. Although he completed high school, he showed no interest in further education. We suggested that he considered military service, and he enlisted in the U.S. Army.

While stationed in Germany he fathered a male child. We only learned about the situation when the mother of his son informed us that we now had a grandson named Jerome. Tony received a dishonorable discharge from the army and left military service and Germany after being involved in a fight with another soldier. After returning to the United States, he never again was in contact with his son or the boy's mother nor with us. Fortunately, we were able to develop a good relationship with Jerome and his mother, Sonja, both of whom attended Robbie's memorial service.

Meanwhile, planning called for the church fundraising campaign to begin its public phase with a kick-off banquet in the grand ballroom of the Hilton hotel on Seventh Avenue. One of the strategy discussions focused upon the need for a keynote speaker who would attract both publicity and a crowd. As the committee considered possible candidates, I suggested Archbishop Desmond Tutu. However, my colleagues seemed to agree that the archbishop was not likely to respond to an invitation from us. When I suggested that I would be willing to approach him, I know that at least some of the committee members were skeptical about my access to the South African prelate and our chances of securing his acceptance. Nonetheless, I was given permission to invite him to speak at our campaign kick-off.

What the committee members did not realize was that I had met Archbishop Tutu, as already described, on several occasions during my travels to South Africa as a church executive; indeed, I had been invited to his enthronement as Bishop of Johannesburg in 1985. The issue was not a lack of personal familiarity.

(At the time, Archbishop Tutu was a scholar in residence at the University of North Florida. The reason for his presence there, rather than at a more prestigious academic institution, was deeply personal and merits brief mention.

Kamele "Oupa" Seane, Director of the <u>Intercultural Center for Peace</u> at the university had invited him. The two men had known each other since they were both teenagers. Years before, Tutu had helped Seane, a young freedom fighter, to escape from South Africa. Their friendship never waned.)

Jim Costen came to my rescue again with some specific recommendations about how best to persuade the archbishop to be our speaker. As a result, when it was time for the banquet, he traveled to New York with his wife and a security aide and received a generous (but not extravagant) speaking honorarium and travel expenses for all of them. Taking my daughter Cassandra with me, I met them at Newark Airport.

On the evening of March 1, 2003, nearly 900 people gathered in the Grand Ballroom of the New York Hilton Hotel for the public launching of the Fifth Avenue Presbyterian Church campaign. The program opened with a beautiful medley of both classical and Broadway selections by excellent musicians. Then Archbishop Tutu began his speech with these remarks:

> *...I have to confess that I agreed to come really only because my old friend Dr. Oscar McCloud asked me. We in South Africa owe him and others like him a huge debt for all the support he gave us during our struggle against the vicious policy of apartheid, particularly when he was a leading light in the World Council of Churches.*

I think it is safe to note that some people's estimates of my clout jumped a few points that evening.

We wrapped up a successful fundraising campaign and the remodeling and expansion of the facilities were completed on schedule. (Tewell, who was fond of preaching sermon series, delivered one set titled "Christians under Construction.") While the 18-month renovation program was underway, we worshiped in nearby Central Synagogue, the beautiful sanctuary of the prominent Reform congregation. The only request that our Jewish neighbors made of us was that we not bring any pork products into the synagogue or leave behind any hymnals. We returned to our own facilities on Easter Sunday of 2004.

Our own congregation continued to grow. We were conducting numerous wedding ceremonies for young couples, and one year, as I recall, we performed 56 baptisms. Our membership became increasingly diverse and inclusive, and Tom Tewell's star continued on the rise; among the honors that came his way was being elected board chair of Princeton Theological Seminary, his alma mater. And then the bubble burst when he and the church parted company after some alleged impropriety in his behavior.

I felt that it was time for me to fulfill my twice-postponed retirement. To allow adequate time for a smooth transition, the Session and I agreed that my final Sunday would be July 1, 2005. During my final months, I was feted at several celebratory events, including a dinner with all of the Trustees and Elders with whom I had worked. After I preached my final sermon, the congregation graciously awarded me the rather rare title of Associate Pastor of Administration Emeritus and presented me with a fishing tackle box that held sufficient funds for several more trips to Alaska.

One more honor awaited me. No sooner had I left the Fifth Avenue church payroll than the Presbytery of New York requested my services as Moderator—a volunteer position that included presiding over quarterly meetings for one year.

Serving as Moderator of the New York Presbytery was for the most part a pleasant experience. It even included an occasion when I persuaded Archbishop Tutu (who was in the city to be honored by Union Theological Seminary) to interrupt his schedule and speak to our organization. Since it was the second time I had successfully prevailed upon the internationally known prelate for his assistance, my reputation climbed several more notches.

However, I also encountered situations when the political maneuvering of church politics left a bad taste in my mouth. One such occasion involved a candidate from another part of the country who was campaigning to become the Moderator of the next General Assembly. This individual sought to strengthen the chances of being chosen by promoting the election of a racial/ethnic representative of our presbytery as a commissioner (and thereby eligible to become a running mate). Our Presbytery's leaders, who already had picked their delegation to the convention, officially rejected the effort to interfere with their decision.

I was thrown one last curve at my final meeting as Moderator of New York Presbytery. That session was supposed to conclude with the installation of Chris Kim as my successor. However, at the last minute Elder Kim learned that the friend he had recruited to preach a sermon for the occasion could not attend. Deeply embarrassed, Elder Kim slipped me a note with the scribbled request that I come to his rescue. I resisted the temptation to decline and used the 45-minute lunch break to pray fervently for divine assistance with a message. The answer I received became a 10-12 minute "sermonette" that some in the audience later described as one of my best—and "shortest"—homilies.

Even after I had fulfilled my Moderator responsibilities, yet another job waited to be done. The Presbytery needed an acting executive while it completed its search for someone more permanent to fill that position. When asked to assist, I accepted the offer. Once again, my office was in the familiar "God Box"—the Interchurch Center at 475 Riverside Drive.

I declined one financially attractive offer of a full-time interim position at a prominent city church, but then another Manhattan congregation approached me with a tempting proposition. That church had received a large gift to underwrite the employment of three seminarians. Now it was looking for someone to design and supervise a program that would train the students in congregational ministry. I accepted the offer, which called for me to meet and confer with them every Wednesday and to observe their roles in leading worship on Sundays.

At the end of the first year, I asked the senior pastor whether he had found my successor. He confessed that he stopped looking for someone, hoping I would continue my duties. I agreed to remain but concluded that working two days each week was not a suitable schedule for enjoying retirement. When my second year of supervising seminarians came to an end, I happily announced my permanent retirement from all official duties.

12

And Then Along Came Kathy

AS I HAVE ALREADY DESCRIBED, my first wife, Robbie, and I met during our high school years at Boggs Academy in Georgia. At the time of her death, we had known each other for 52 years and had been married for 42 of them. Our many achievements included raising a family together. As her final illness moved toward its end, I reached the firm conclusion that I would never marry again. My reasoning was simple: the relationship with Robbie had developed over many years from our youth and was too involved for me to imagine adjusting to another spouse and subjecting her to comparison with my first wife.

It was not easy for me to recover from Robbie's decade-long decline in health and then death. To be sure, it helped me to have a deeply dependent daughter who required a great deal of attention. For most of the next decade, though, I lived alone as a widower and adjusted to that lifestyle. I dated other women but was quick to inform them that I intended to remain single—a declaration that usually brought those relationships to an end. I also was firm in sharing that same attitude with my immediate family and close friends.

Then in 2010 I went to the Presbyterian Church General Assembly in Minneapolis as one of many volunteers. Some of us who were providing staff services to several of the Assembly committees were seated together in the convention hall. Kathy Walker had been assigned a place near me. When I struck up a conversation with her, I learned she was from St. Petersburg, Florida—not very far from the group home in which my daughter Michelle was living.

After exchanging pleasantries, she and I agreed to continue our conversation over dinner while we were still in Minneapolis. By the time the Assembly was over, we had exchanged email addresses and phone numbers and agreed to see each other again during one of my trips to visit Michelle. Soon thereafter Kathy invited me to escort her to a wedding in New Jersey to which she had been invited.

By this time I knew a lot more about my new friend—her family, her history, her "likes" and "dislikes". She had been born in Columbus, Georgia (the middle child of three siblings), and raised in Northwest Atlanta. She attended Dixie Hill Elementary School, Herndon Elementary School, and Booker T. Washington High School and graduated from Frederick Douglass High School. Being enrolled in the federally sponsored Upward Bound program was her stepping stone to Florida Presbyterian (now Eckerd) College in St. Petersburg, Florida. There she met and married Walter Walker. After his graduation, she followed him to Clemson University where he entered the Ph.D program. Kathy earned her bachelor's and master's degrees in elementary education at Clemson, and after returning to Florida, embarked on a 35-year career as a teacher and administrator in the Pinellas County school system.

When I met her in Minneapolis she had been divorced for 11 years and had two grown daughters. From the beginning of our relationship, I tried to make it clear to her that I had no interest in returning to a state of matrimony. Nevertheless, as we continued to see each other, it was clear that we were forming a mutual interest in each other. After a year of sporadic commuting to spend time together in Florida and New Jersey, I had to admit to myself that I was succumbing to Kathy's charm. I also had to concede that my brave claims about having been alone but not lonely were statements of self-deception.

During a trip together to Bar Harbor, Maine during the summer of 2011 I proposed to Kathy on the summit of Cadillac Mountain in Acadia National Park and presented her with an engagement ring.

Our initial two-year plan called for us to live in New Jersey while we looked for a home in Atlanta that would put us closer to our Georgia-based families. The next February, while visiting some of those relatives, I took Kathy to see a new townhouse development in southwest Atlanta, close to the area where I had lived during the 1960s. The gate to the community was locked, so we could only peer through the fence at the attractive compound. However, Kathy's further research identified a few vacant units. We decided that she should return to Atlanta and examine them more closely. After she identified one that appealed to her, I was sufficiently convinced to return to Atlanta from New Jersey and look it over too.

Our wedding was still several months away, but I was persuaded that we should purchase the property. Consequently, within a matter of weeks, we each still owned a home and had also purchased a townhouse together. Fortunately, Kathy succeeded in selling her Florida residence and moving her furniture to our new but unoccupied Atlanta property by the time of our wedding. Then we owned *only* two residences.

We were married on May 26, 2012 at the Hilton Hotel in St. Petersburg, Florida, with more than one hundred family members and friends present to help us celebrate.

We returned to Teaneck to consider next steps. However, Hurricane Sandy hit New Jersey in late October, leaving us without central heating. We slept beside our wood-burning fireplace for a week. Since we owned an empty townhouse in Atlanta, it was not a difficult decision to vacate New Jersey. Our two-year plan rapidly shrunk to a six-month schedule.

By mid-November we had packed up and moved to our new home in Southwest Atlanta.

We quickly became involved in local affairs and rejoiced at being closer to our Georgia families. After visiting several congregations, we chose Central Presbyterian Church in downtown Atlanta as the worship community in which we felt most welcome. I already was acquainted with this progressive fellowship and the civil rights leadership of its former pastor, the Rev. Dr. J. Randolph Taylor, from the 1960s. Kathy was especially attracted to the church's music, arts program, and its women's circle. I further chose to become active in the leadership of our homeowners' association.

We also embarked upon a series of cruises—to the Caribbean, Central America, and Europe. Our most exciting voyage was a visit to the Norwegian fjords. In 2013, at the invitation of the Office of the General Assembly of the Presbyterian Church, we spent four weeks in South Africa where I served on a mediation team for the Presbyterian Church of South Africa and also traveled around the country.

Our happy lifestyle was interrupted in 2014 when we learned that I had prostate cancer and, two years later, that Kathy required the replacement of two heart valves. Fortunately for both of us, there were no negative side effects from the procedures to correct those conditions. However, we began to realize that our bodies were being challenged by the constant climbing of stairs in a four-level townhouse. Our search for another residence yielded the discovery of an available property in the Buckhead district of Atlanta. Situated on the fourth floor of a beautifully landscaped condominium property, it could be reached by an elevator and offered a view of the city. We moved quickly to acquire it as our new home.

Times spent with our blended family of four adult daughters, two sons-in-law, and two grandsons help to keep us occupied, as does our involvement with Central Presbyterian. Kathy has served as a Deacon and frequently is called upon to be a lector during Sunday morning worship services and other occasions. I recently recruited a group of Central men to prepare and serve some of their favorite dishes for a fundraising luncheon on behalf of the church's Outreach and Advocacy Center.

Kathy and I have been married for more than 14 years. It has been one of the happiest periods of my life. We continue to celebrate the joy of our partnership and the richness of family relations and retirement—grateful to God for the journey that led us to each other.

CONCLUSION

As I sort through my memories, my wife, Kathy, and I are living in the Buckhead section of Atlanta. Our fourth-floor condominium overlooking Peachtree Street is a far cry from the crude shanty in which I was born on a plantation in rural Georgia. I clearly have come a long way.

Ninety years ago in a remote corner of rural Georgia I received the gift of life . The only promise that came with it was the possibility that I might survive long enough to earn a lifetime pittance for picking cotton. However, something that I can only attribute to the grace of God intervened and set my feet on a different route—one that offered me the joyful opportunity to be of service.

Throughout my nine decades I have been blessed and guided by the instruction and example of many other leaders. Because of their example and equipped with a good education and the urge to promote justice, I found myself called to positions of leadership in Georgia, in the South, in the United States, and, indeed, in the world.

Undergirding my progress from a cotton field to positions of leadership in the worldwide Protestant church have been the support and encouragement of hundreds of men and women who themselves have helped to bring about positive change all over the earth. My exposure to them has brought me enormous peace and joy and deepened my understanding of what it means to build the human community.

To God be the glory.

A Guide to Presbyterianism

A PRESBYTERIAN IS A PROTESTANT WHO favors a representative form of church government.

A Presbyterian Church is governed by two types of elders: Teaching Elders (who are ordained ministers with responsibility for preaching, teaching, and administering the two sacraments of communion and baptism) and Ruling Elders (who are elected from the church membership) with responsibility for leadership and governance.

Ruling Elders, with the minister/Teaching Elder at their head as Moderator, form the "Session," a governing body with authority in all spiritual matters of the local church.

Congregations also have boards of deacons and of trustees. Deacons generally have responsibility for promoting visitation and fellowship among the members, while trustees have responsibility for the legal and financial affairs of the congregation.

A presbytery is a regional group of churches, represented by their Teaching and Ruling Elders.

A synod is a larger regional group of several presbyteries.

A General Assembly is the highest governing body of the Presbyterian denomination with representation of all its presbyteries.

Rather than relying upon the decisions of individual leaders like bishops, Presbyterians depend upon the collective decision-making of Elders, who in turn believe that Christ is the ultimate head of the church.

ACKNOWLEDGEMENTS

I AM GRATEFUL FOR THE ASSISTANCE of David Staniunas, Records Archivist and Assistant Stated Clerk, PC (USA), Presbyterian Historical Society.

Special appreciation goes to my co-author, Martin Lehfeldt. He knew the questions to ask that helped me to arrange my memories and articulate my thoughts and ideas. Without his assistance, this book would never have been completed.

Many thanks to the publishing team at Ripples Media who took the words of this manuscript and transformed it into a book that readers can hold.

My wife, Kathy, patiently tolerated the many hours during which I deserted her to spend time at my computer, and generously read and shared her opinions of my drafts.

ABOUT THE AUTHOR

THE REV. J. OSCAR McCLOUD is Associate Pastor emeritus at Fifth Avenue Presbyterian Church in New York City, where he served as an administrative pastor from 1995 to 2005.

In addition to his congregational work, he has served in a number of leadership roles for the Presbyterian Church. Before coming to Fifth Avenue Presbyterian Church, he was the Executive Director of The Fund for Theological Education for nine years from 1987 to 1994. Most recently, he served as the moderator of the Presbytery of New York City from 2005 to 2006, and also as the Acting Executive Presbyter for the

Presbytery of New York City, which serves as the regional body of the Presbyterian Church (USA).

Oscar was first ordained into Christian ministry in 1961 and received a call as pastor of Davie Presbyterian Church in Raleigh, North Carolina, where he served for three years. Later, from 1964 to 1971, he was on staff at the United Presbyterian Church, working with civil rights groups across the Southeast.

Over his career, Oscar has traveled extensively on behalf of the Presbyterian Church, including trips to Europe, Africa, Asia, as well as Central and South America. He was active in the anti-apartheid movement in the US and Southern Africa. He met Nelson Mandela at his home in Soweto in 1990 when he was in South Africa for the multi-racial Rustenburg Conference of religious leaders. More recently, he and his wife Kathy spent a month in South Africa in 2013 where he was a member of the mediation team with the United Presbyterian Church in Southern Africa.

He has been active in his local community, serving on the Board of Trustees of Englewood Hospital (New Jersey), the chair of the Teaneck (New Jersey) Advisory Board on Community Relations, as well as the Board of Trustees at Berea College and TransAfrica, an anti-apartheid lobby in Washington, DC.

He has received a number of awards, including the Congressional Black Caucus Religious Leader award, Berea College Community Service Award, and the Warren Wilson College outstanding alumni award.

Oscar and his wife Robbie were high school sweethearts and married in 1960. They were married forty-two years, with two daughters Michelle and Cassandra. Robbie passed away in 2002.

Oscar married his wife Kathleen Walker in 2012. Together, they have a blended family of four adult daughters. Today, he and Kathy live in Atlanta and are members of Central Presbyterian Church.

I Dared to Hope is Oscar's first book, with its launch in April 2026 coinciding with his ninetieth birthday.